DOG HIKING NORTHERN CALIFORNIA

42 Unmissable Dog-Friendly Trails

HELVETIQ publishing is being supported by the Swiss Federal Office of Culture with a structural grant for the years 2026–2028.

Dog Hiking Northern California
42 Unmissable Dog-Friendly Trails

Authors and photographers: © Melissa Chen
Cover design: Ajša Zdravković
Illustrations, typesetting and layout: Elżbieta Kownacka
Editor: Johanna Flashman
Proofreader: Theresa Cameron

ISBN: 978-3-03964-103-1
First edition: 2026
Printed in China

We are grateful to Livia Waser for her work on Dog Hiking Switzerland.

Mittlere Strasse 4
4056 Basel
Switzerland

DOG HIKING NORTHERN CALIFORNIA

42 Unmissable Dog-Friendly Trails

By Melissa Chen

TABLE OF CONTENTS

IMPORTANT INFORMATION

HOW I SELECTED THE HIKES

With decades of experience hiking in Northern California, I created this guide with my own dogs of different athletic abilities (a water-loving chocolate lab and a short-statured basset hound). I understand how hiking together can deepen the bond between you and your dog.

I chose hikes not too far from major areas that are worth it for you both, and hikes that can be integrated into a vacation. I discovered quiet trails, water to swim in, open summits, off-leash trails, and plenty of hidden gems—and I'm sharing my favorites with you! These 42 carefully selected hikes were chosen for their beauty, accessibility and dog-friendly policies.

Recognizing that each dog is different in ability and energy, I've included scenic hikes for dogs of all ages and challenging terrain for more adventurous pups. I spoke to locals while out on these trails to deliver the best insider knowledge. My hope is that these trails help you and your dog explore and find joy in the simple act of hiking together. Have fun!

HIKE PREPARATION

Being well prepared is a must when hiking with dogs, no matter the hike's length or difficulty. You'll need a good daypack to hold gear for both you and your dog. Here are some items to consider for a safe and enjoyable hike.

1. **Navigation:** The GPX files I used for the maps are for reference only. A paper map and compass, and knowing how to use them, are the most reliable navigation tools. Phone batteries can die, and there's no guarantee when using technology in the wilderness. Packing a backup charger helps, but be prepared to hike without your phone.

2. **Hydration:** Remember to pack ample water for you and your dog, relative to the hike distance and weather conditions. The recommendation for moderate hikes is a half-liter of water per hour for humans and 0.25 ounces per pound per hour for dogs—so a 40-pound dog needs 10 ounces for an hour-long hike. For hot temperatures and strenuous hikes, double these amounts. Bring a collapsible bowl so your dog can drink easily.

3. **Food:** Packing adequate, high-calorie food like protein bars and trail mix will provide enough fuel to sustain energy levels during an active hike. Dogs need extra calories while hiking, just like we do, so it may make sense to feed them larger meal portions on hike days. Carry extra snacks in case you find yourselves away from home longer than planned.

4. **Clothing:** Layering is key for hiking in Northern California, as weather can change quickly and temperatures fluctuate significantly with elevation. It's important to have rain and wind gear, plus extra layers of insulation, including a hat and gloves. Wear a moisture-wicking base layer and wool or wool-blend socks, which stay warm

even if they get wet. For hiking in snow and cold temperatures with your pup, consider packing a dog vest and booties for extra warmth.

5. **First aid:** Carrying a first aid kit and having basic first-aid knowledge is crucial, since injuries can happen on any hike. Every kit should include moleskin for blisters, tweezers for tick removal, and bandages and biodegradable soap for cleaning wounds. The American Red Cross offers human and pet first-aid online training and an app: redcross.org/take-a-class/first-aid/cat-dog-first-aid

6. **Lights:** Packing a headlamp (plus spare batteries) for you and a collar light for your dog is a must for hikes of all durations. Hikes can take longer than planned, and getting caught in the dark is always a possibility—especially on a sunset hike.

7. **Sun protection:** Apply sunscreen before a hike and pack it with you or wear sun-protective clothing—exposed trails can quickly lead to sunburn. Pack a broad-brimmed hat and sunglasses, too.

8. **Insect protection:** Ticks can be a challenge in this region. Ticks exist year-round but are most active from March through July. Wearing light-colored long pants and sleeves can reduce your risk of being bitten by a tick. Applying permethrin to clothing and gear will provide an extra layer of protection against ticks. Permethrin is considered safe for dogs, but never apply it to their fur, skin, or face—it should only be used on gear. The most reliable protection against ticks is a thorough check after every hike.

9. **Sanitation:** Proper waste disposal protects water sources, wildlife, and the beauty of natural spaces. If you need to pee or poop in the woods, go at least 200 feet away from any trail or water source. Bury human waste in a six-inch-deep cathole or carry it out. Dog waste and toilet paper should be carried out, so pack those plastic dog-poop bags.

10. **Fire starter and shelter:** If you're on a difficult hike in challenging terrain, carry matches in a waterproof container, along with some fast-burning birch bark as a potential heat source. Warmth is invaluable if you and your dog are lost. Plus, pack an emergency blanket or small tarp for shelter in case of an emergency overnight stay.

CREATING THE MAPS

Maps in this book were created using Gaia GPS. With a paid Gaia GPS membership, you can download maps ahead of time and access them offline without an internet connection. Once downloaded, you'll be able to open that map via Gaia GPS and use the app's built-in GPS tracking to follow your location in real time—even without cell service.

The app will show you where you are on the trail, so you can easily tell if you're on track, need to make a turn, or should retrace your steps. It's a great way to explore with peace of mind, knowing you're on the right path.

HIKING WITH YOUR DOG

Hiking with dogs is endlessly rewarding and can provide both of you with an incredible bonding experience. These tips can help make it even better.

1. **Research each hike beforehand:** Before setting out on any hike, consider your pet's health and fitness level, and the trail distance, elevation gain, and difficulty. Be aware of potential obstacles, like rock scrambles or wooden ladders.

2. **Start with short, simple hikes:** If you're both new to hiking, work up to longer hikes by building endurance and confidence on shorter, easier routes.

3. **Avoid hiking in unsafe temperatures:** Anything below 20 or above 80 degrees F is considered unsafe for hiking with dogs. Even temperatures above 65 degrees can be risky for larger or older dogs, depending on the terrain. Consider hiking during cooler times of the day.

4. **Understand your dog's limits:** Pack plenty of snacks and water, take frequent breaks, seek shade, and pay attention to signs of distress or injury, such as excessive panting, drooling, lethargy, limping, shivering, or disorientation.

5. **Maintain vaccinations and tick prevention:** Heartworm and flea/tick prevention are crucial for hiking dogs. Always check dogs for ticks after each hike, especially on their bellies, legs, ears, and face.

6. **ID tag:** Include your name and phone number in case you get separated.

7. **Obedience training:** Make sure your dog knows basic commands, like "come" and "stay," and walks easily on a leash.

LEASH LAWS

The majority of hiking trails require dogs be leashed or, at the very least, under voice command. In this book, I've noted a small handful of trails that are approved off-leash areas—they're clearly marked in each relevant chapter.

You can also refer to the land manager's website for the most up-to-date information. Regardless of the leash laws, be ready to leash your dog when you come across another dog or hiker on trail; not everyone is fond of dogs, so this is for everyone's comfort.

WEATHER AND SEASONS

Northern California has diverse microclimates with local conditions, and it's important to check and re-check the forecast before setting out on a hike. Always be prepared for wind, rain, and snow on hikes with higher elevation—even in the summer. Before heading out, check the National Weather Service for an accurate forecast: forecast.weather.gov. For high-elevation peaks, use mountain-forecast.com for more accurate alpine predictions.

Spring and late fall are ideal times to hike, thanks to milder temperatures and smaller crowds compared to the summer, although each season has its own appeal. In spring, highlights include blooming wildflowers and flowing streams, despite the increased chance of rain and mud. Fall offers cooler temperatures and changing leaves. Summer provides extra daylight for longer hikes and opportunities for swimming in lakes, streams, and waterfalls. Seasoned hikers with the right gear enjoy the quiet solitude and snow-covered trees during winter hikes. Always check for trail updates in winter, as access roads might be closed. Some coastal areas, like redwood forests, maintain mild temperatures year-round and offer excellent hiking in any season.

TRAIL ETIQUETTE

1. **Stay on trail:** This will reduce erosion and damage to fragile flora. If there's mud on the trail, walk through it, not around it. Try to keep your dog on trail, too.

2. **Limit group sizes:** Groups larger than ten people can be hard on the environment and cause a negative experience for other hikers. When hiking in a large group, consider splitting into smaller groups and choosing meetup spots along the way and after the hike.

3. **Leave no trace:** Leave rocks, plants, and other discoveries undisturbed. Always take plastic bags (and plenty of dog poop bags) to pack out your garbage.

4. **Respect wildlife:** Observe wildlife from a distance and never feed wild animals. Keep dogs on leash when encountering other animals on a hike.

5. **Yield to other hikers:** Uphill hikers have the right-of-way, and people hiking with dogs should always yield, regardless of the direction they're hiking. Move entirely off the trail to give other hikers space to pass.

6. **Be considerate of others:** Hike quietly, kindly greet other hikers, and offer to help when needed.

7. **Park responsibly:** If the trailhead is full when you arrive, consider returning later or on another day, or look for an alternative legal space.

HUNTING

National Forest and Bureau of Land Management lands generally permit hunting from September to January, depending on the game animal and region. Check local forest alerts or contact ranger stations for current hunting activity before you head out. During hunting season, always wear orange safety clothing and put your dog in an orange safety vest or bandana.

PUBLIC TRANSPORT

You'll have to drive to most of the hikes in Northern California, as public transportation doesn't reach the remote areas. Cell service may also be limited at the trailhead, and you may not be able to call a taxi or Uber. Check each hike's chapter and the land manager's website for parking fees or required reservations. Some trailheads only accept cash and don't provide change.

PARKING

Each hike explains how to get to the trailhead by car and where to park.

FURTHER RESOURCES

For hiking accommodation, BringFido is a directory of pet-friendly hotels and dog travel: bringfido.com.

Region	Type	Website
Bay Area		
	Hiking	bahiker.com
Marin County		
	Visitor Amenities	visitmarin.org
San Francisco		
	Visitor Amenities	sftravel.com
Peninsula		
	Visitor Amenities	thesanfranciscopeninsula.com
Silicon Valley		
	Visitor Amenities	visitsiliconvalley.org sanjose.org visitmorganhill.org discoversantaclara.org

East Bay

Visitor Amenities	visitoakland.com visitberkeley.com

Santa Cruz and Monterey

Visitor Amenities	seemonterey.com santacruz.org
Hiking	santacruztrails.org mprpd.org

Yosemite & Sierra Nevada Foothills

Visitor Amenities	travelyosemite.com stancounty.com visitmurphys.com californiahighsierra.com
Hiking	highsierratopix.com tahoetrailguide.com

Lake Tahoe & Desolation Wilderness

Visitor Amenities	visitlaketahoe.com californiahighsierra.com
Hiking	highsierratopix.com tahoetrailguide.com

Greater Sacramento

Visitor Amenities	visitsacramento.com visitdavis.org visitfolsom.com nevadacitychamber.com visitplacer.com
Hiking	northerncaliforniahikingtrails.com

Shasta County

Visitor Amenities	visitmtshasta.com
Hiking	hikemtshasta.com mountshastatrailassociation.org

Mendocino Coast

Visitor Amenities	visitmendocino.com
Hiking	mendocinolandtrust.org/trail-guide

COMMON FLOWERS

1. **California Poppy.** California poppy is the state flower, with orange cup-shaped blooms that close at night and reopen in morning sunlight. Its "fields of gold" flowers are reminiscent of the Gold Rush period. Native American tribes used the California poppy for food and medicine, including for toothaches and to promote sleep. They bloom from February to September, with peak blooms from March to May. They're most commonly found in grasslands, coastal bluffs, and open meadows, like in Mount Tamalpais State Park.

2. **Sky Lupine.** Sky lupine is a native plant with tall spikes of purple or blue flowers arranged in dense vertical clusters. You can sometimes find variations with white flowers. They bloom from March to May. They're most commonly found in coastal prairies, grasslands, and oak woodlands, like at Beeks Bight in Folsom Lake.

3. **Blue Dicks.** Blue dicks is a native wildflower with clusters of small blue to purple funnel-shaped flowers on long, leafless stems. You can occasionally find variations with pink-purple or white flowers. Native Americans ate blue dicks corms (underground plant stems), and some tribes like the Miwok harvested them like a crop. They bloom from March to May and are most commonly found in grasslands, oak woodlands, and serpentine soils, like on the Quarry Trail.

4. **Indian Paintbrush.** Indian paintbrush is a native wildflower with bright red, orange, or yellow tubular flowers that resemble a paintbrush. Some Native American tribes ate the flowers in moderation, but not the toxic leaves and roots. They bloom from March to June and are most commonly found on hills and mountain slopes, like on the Duchess Mine Trail.

5. **Monkey Flower.** Monkey flower is a native wildflower with five fused petals that vaguely resemble a monkey's face. Variations come in yellow, orange, red, and white flowers. Native American tribes like the Coast Miwok used monkey flower leaves on sores and burns. They bloom from March to September and are most commonly found in chaparral, coastal scrub, and woodlands at low elevations, like in Folsom Lake.

6. **Tidy Tips.** Tidy tips are a native wildflower with yellow daisy-like flowers and petals that are white around the edges. The Ohlone peoples would ground the seeds into powder and eat them with mush or porridge. They bloom from March to July. They're most commonly found in grasslands, coastal prairies, and open fields, like in Tilden Regional Park. Foresters may use tidy tips in grassland restoration projects because the flower attracts bees, butterflies, and birds.

7. **Seaside Daisy.** Seaside daisy is a native perennial plant with lavender-pink flowers and large, yellow centers. They have a long blooming season from April to October, with peak blooms from May to August. They're most commonly found on coastal bluffs, beaches, and dunes, like in Mendocino Headlands State Park.

8. **Golden Yarrow.** Golden yarrow is a native shrub with clusters of small yellow daisy-like flowers. Golden yarrow attracts butterflies, bees, and other pollinators. They bloom from March to August. They're most commonly found in woodlands or shrublands, south of the San Francisco Bay Area and inland in the Sierra Nevadas.

9. **Pacific Coast Iris.** Pacific Coast iris is a native wildflower with purple, blue, or white flowers featuring three upright petals. Native American tribes used iris fibers to create rope and baskets. Some tribes also dried Douglas iris roots (a subspecies of Pacific Coast iris) to make a diuretic. They bloom from March to May. They're most commonly found in coastal grasslands, oak woodlands, and forest edges, like on Mount Tamalpais.

10. **Bluewitch Nightshade.** Bluewitch nightshade is a native California shrub with purple star-shaped flowers and bright-yellow anthers. They bloom from January to September, with peak blooming from April to July. They're most commonly found in chaparral and low-elevation oak woodlands, like in Almaden Quicksilver County Park.

INDIGENOUS ACKNOWLEDGEMENTS

The trails in this book sit on the ancestral territories of Indigenous peoples who have lived here for thousands of years. From the Coast Miwok and Ohlone peoples of the Bay Area to the Washoe and Maidu nations around Lake Tahoe, Native communities called Northern California home and continue to develop deep knowledge of these lands.

Many of the lands in Northern California were stolen from Native American tribes through forced removal and colonization. As you hike these trails with your dogs, we encourage you to learn about the Indigenous history of each area and support ongoing Native-led conservation efforts.

MAP AND HIKE INDEX

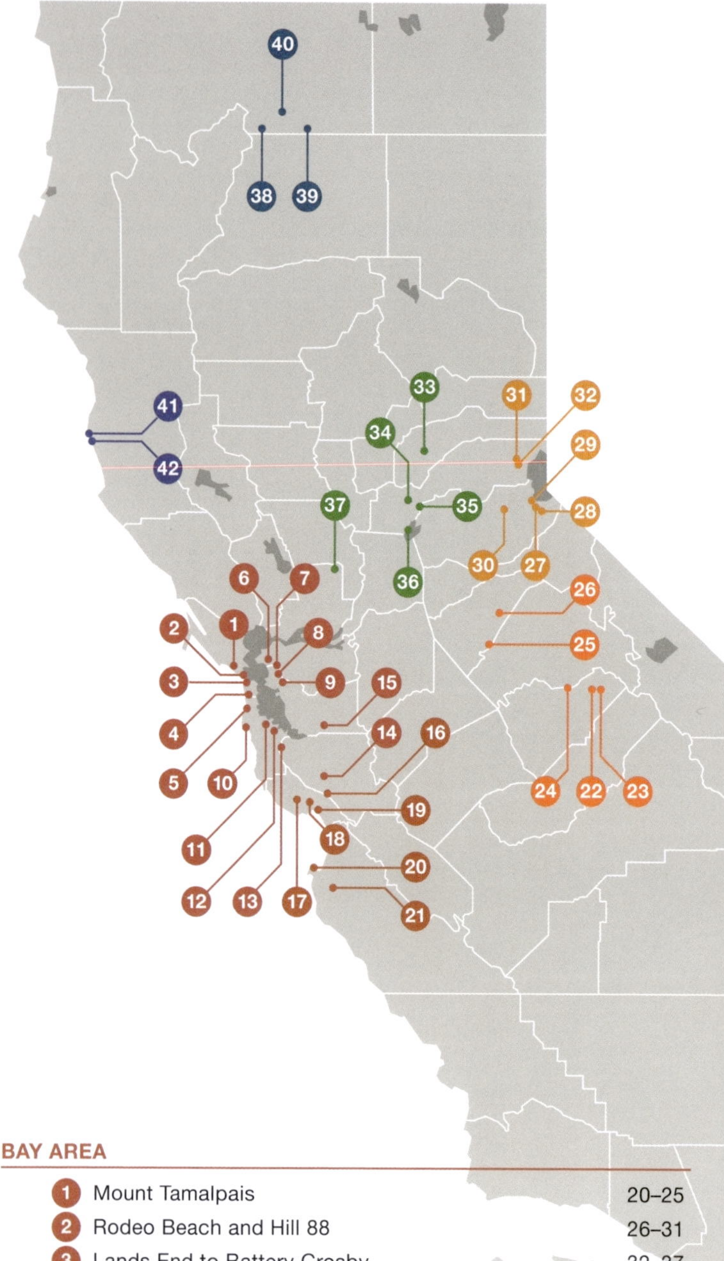

BAY AREA

BAY AREA

STINSON BEACH

MARIN CITY

1 2 3 4 5 6 7 8 9 10

P Parking

Bench

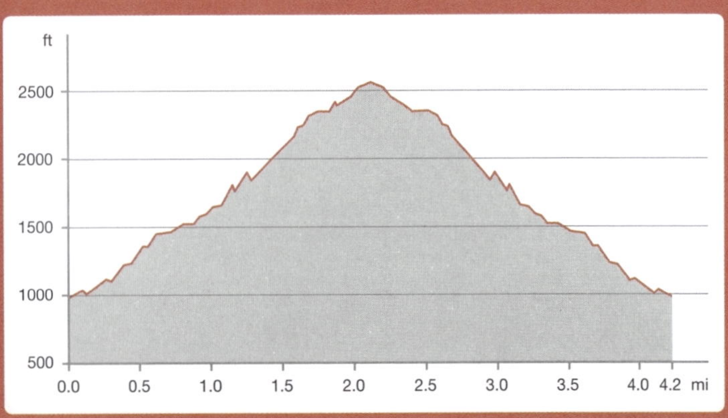

MOUNT TAMALPAIS

HIKE TO MOUNT TAM'S EAST PEAK

MILL VALLEY, CA

1

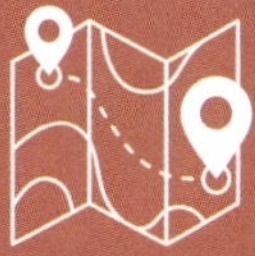

LENGTH
4.2 miles (loop)

TIME & MONEY
2 hours 30 min., free

ELEVATION GAIN
1,510 feet

DIFFICULTY
Strenuous

CONDITIONS
Year-round; partially exposed

HIGHLIGHTS
Panoramic views

ESSENTIALS

- **Find the trailhead:** From San Francisco, take US-101 Northbound and cross the Golden Gate Bridge. In 7.2 miles, take the exit for CA-1 toward Mill Valley/Stinson Beach. In 0.2 miles, continue on CA-1. In 0.8 miles, turn left to stay on CA-1. In 2.6 miles, take a slight right onto the Panoramic Highway. In 2.5 miles, the parking lot will be on your left. The parking lot is across the street from the Mountain Home Inn.
- **Land manager:** California State Parks (parks.ca.gov)

WHY YOU'LL LOVE IT

- Sweeping views of Marin and the San Francisco Bay
- Fun and challenging trail
- Dog-friendly section on a local's favorite: "Mount Tam"

A drive through rolling hills and coastal fog takes you to a challenging but short climb to the East Peak of Mount Tamalpais. At the top, you'll enjoy views of the San Francisco Bay and surrounding area.

Mount Tamalpais, affectionately called "Mount Tam" by locals, is an icon in the Bay Area outdoor scene. Sitting at 2,500 feet, Mount Tam is one of the best hiking destinations in Marin because of its breathtaking views, lengthy network of trails, and diverse ecosystem. While not all of Mount Tam allows dogs, the hike to East Peak is a dog-friendly hiking trail option.

The name Tamalpais is closely related to the Coast Miwok name for this mountain, támal pájiṣ, which literally means "west hill." The Coast Miwok are Indigenous people who lived in what is now Marin and southern Sonoma County. They lived in the area for thousands of years, hunting and gathering on the bountiful land.

When you reach the parking lot for the trailhead, you'll be parked across from the famous Mountain Home Inn. Established in 1912, the Mountain Home Inn was once a famous stop along the Mount Tam railway route. Because of its historic status, it was grandfathered in as the only commercial property on the mountain.

Your hike up to the East Peak starts on an unmarked dirt fire road. While the ascent is fairly straightforward, the descent that you will make on your return can be a bit slippery, as the small rocks making up the trail are loose. As you head up the road into the mountains, you may see or hear birds such as the red-tailed hawk or peregrine falcon. Peregrine falcons are incredible hunters—they have been recorded reaching speeds of up to 242 miles per hour and can spot prey from over 10,000 feet away. The Mount Tam area is home to many species that thrive in the temperate climate.

After a mile and a half on a steady incline, you'll first cross another parking lot (cars can drive all the way up to the East Peak trailhead base) before your final climb up the last half mile or so. Here, you can read the interpretive display about Mount Tam, take a short detour to the Gravity Car Museum, or continue up to the peak. The museum displays historic memorabilia of the Mount Tam railway, which ran from the 1800s to the early 1900s, known as the "Crookedest Railroad in the World." Because of the steep hills and landscape of Mount Tam, the railway had to navigate 281 curves. One of the sections was named the "Double Bow Knot," because the track paralleled itself five times within 200 yards. The museum is staffed by volunteers but is typically open on weekend afternoons.

At the top of East Peak, you'll see the Gardner Fire Lookout. Built between 1935 and 1936, it's still an active fire lookout today. You can carefully tread around the edge to see spectacular views of Marin, the Golden Gate Bridge, and the rest of the Bay Area below.

TURN-BY-TURN DIRECTIONS

1. From the trailhead, take the unmarked dirt road to your left.
2. At 0.2 miles, you'll see Throckmorton Fire Station on your right. Continue straight on the dirt trail.
3. At 0.4 miles, continue straight at the marked junction toward East Peak.
4. At 0.5 miles, continue straight at the marked junction toward East Peak.
5. At 0.6 miles, turn left at the junction onto the signposted Railroad Grade Fire Road.
6. At 1.0 mile, turn right onto the signposted single track Fern Creek Trail.
7. At 1.3 miles, pass the tavern pump on your right and continue straight at the signpost toward "E. Peak."
8. At 1.6 miles, cross the street at the junction signposted for East Peak and continue up a short set of stairs.
9. At 1.7 miles, arrive at the East Peak parking lot. Turn right and go straight through to the end of the parking lot toward the restrooms. Head up a wooden platform at the signed junction for the "East Peak Summit Fire Lookout." The optional detour to the Gravity Car Museum is 300 feet to your left.
10. At 2.1 miles, reach East Peak. When you're ready, head back the same way you came to the parking lot.

8
6
7
Hill 88
5
4
P
SAUSALITO
3
2
1
10
9
P Parking
Picnic table
Hill 88
Toilet
ft
2500
2000
1500
1000
500
0
0.0
0.5
1.0
1.5
2.0
2.5
3.0
3.5
4.0
4.5
5.2 mi

RODEO BEACH AND HILL 88

COASTAL VIEWS AND HISTORIC LANDMARKS

MARIN COUNTY, CA

2

LENGTH
5.2 miles (loop)

TIME & MONEY
2 hours 15 min., free

ELEVATION GAIN
877 feet

DIFFICULTY
Moderate

CONDITIONS
Year-round; exposed, coastal weather

HIGHLIGHTS
Coastal views, Battery Townsley

ESSENTIALS

- **Find the trailhead:** From San Francisco, take US-101/Presidio Parkway across the Golden Gate Bridge. After crossing the Golden Gate Bridge, continue 0.6 miles on US-101 northbound and then take the exit onto Alexander Avenue. In 0.3 miles, turn left onto Bunker Road. In 3.1 miles, continue straight onto Mitchell Road. In 0.4 miles, the parking lot will be on your right.
- **Land manager:** Golden Gate National Recreation Area (nps.gov/goga)

WHY YOU'LL LOVE IT

- Historic sites and interpretive displays
- Sweeping views of the Pacific Ocean and Rodeo Beach
- Temperate coastal climate year-round
- Dog-friendly Rodeo Beach

Climb up a coastal trail to a historic site from the Cold War. From the site, enjoy expansive views of the Pacific Ocean and the dog-friendly Rodeo Beach down below.

Your hike begins at Rodeo Beach in the Golden Gate National Recreation Area. You may recognize the Golden Gate National Recreation Area, as the park has over 250 trails across 140 miles of land from Marin to San Mateo and is named after the Golden Gate strait, across which the iconic Golden Gate Bridge spans. The park welcomes over 17 million visitors a year!

Rodeo Beach, a favorite local dog-friendly beach, is located at the northern end of the Golden Gate National Recreation Area boundary in Marin, just a few miles after crossing the Golden Gate Bridge. You and your pup can enjoy the beach either before or after your hike. You may also see beachgoers exploring the beach's unique red and green pebbles, flying kites, or surfing in the water.

Your hike from Rodeo Beach up to Hill 88 takes you past Battery Townsley. From 1940 to 1948, Battery Townsley had two 16-inch guns that were designed to guard against enemy ships. Although Battery Townsley is only open to visitors the first Sunday of the month, Gun #386 stands in front of the entrance and is accessible year-round.

Gun #386 is a 16-inch gun that was aboard the battleship USS *Missouri* when the Japanese surrendered in 1945. These guns could fire 2,100-pound projectiles up to 25 miles out, which was a big feat in military engineering at the time. However, by the end of World War II, long-range bombers and nuclear weapons made these types of guns obsolete, and they were scrapped in late 1948. Today, Gun #386 is a reminder of the stories and devastating history of World War II.

Once you leave Gun #386, you're only a mile away from reaching Hill 88. Hill 88 provides a spectacular view out to San Francisco, across the Marin Headlands, and down to Rodeo Beach below. From August to November, you may also see eagles, hawks, falcons, and vultures (birds collectively called "raptors") flying around Hill 88 during their fall migration. Over 19 species have been counted in the area, but the most common raptor species are turkey vultures, red-tailed hawks, Cooper's hawks, and sharp-shinned hawks. Bring a pair of binoculars to help you spot these majestic birds of prey.

You'll also see abandoned structures on Hill 88 dating from the Cold War era. Nike missiles were designed in the 1950s to protect cities like San Francisco from enemy aircraft by shooting them down mid-air. At Hill 88, radar systems tracked incoming threats and guided these missiles. Now, the structures are not actively maintained and are unsafe to enter, so be sure to observe them from the outside only.

The rest of your hike is a gentle descent down the Miwok Trail and a flat traverse on the Lagoon Trail across Rodeo Lagoon, back to the Rodeo Beach parking lot. In Rodeo Lagoon, you may see fish, river otters, and different types of birds like the American coot, egrets, and ducks. Dogs are not allowed to swim here in order to protect the endangered tidewater goby, a small fish that rarely exceeds 2 inches in length. Habitat loss, the introduction of non-native predators, and climate change have all contributed to their decreasing population.

TURN-BY-TURN DIRECTIONS

1. From the parking lot, head through the yellow gates and onto the signposted Coastal Trail, heading north. After 400 feet, at the sign for the Coastal Trail, turn left and begin the hike.
2. At 0.2 miles, stay right for 50 feet, then turn left at the sign for the Coastal Trail.
3. At 0.6 miles, turn left to continue on the marked Coastal Trail. After 50 feet, turn right at the sign to continue on the Coastal Trail toward the Wolf Ridge Trail.
4. At 0.9 miles, turn right onto the unmarked paved trail.
5. At 1.1 miles, stay right to continue on the Coastal Trail.
6. At 1.6 miles, continue straight toward Hill 88 (marked). 950 feet ahead, reach Hill 88. When you're ready, head back 950 feet to the Coastal Trail. Make a sharp right at the sign onto the Wolf Ridge Trail toward the Miwok Trail.
7. At 2.8 miles, turn right at the signage onto the Miwok Trail.
8. At 3.9 miles, continue right on the Miwok Trail.
9. At 4.4 miles, cross the road and turn right at the sign onto the Lagoon Trail, toward Rodeo Beach.
10. At 5.2 miles, arrive back at the parking lot.

9 10
8
7
6
5
3 4
1 2
P
SAUSALITO
GOLDEN GATE PARK
DALY CITY

P Parking

Bench

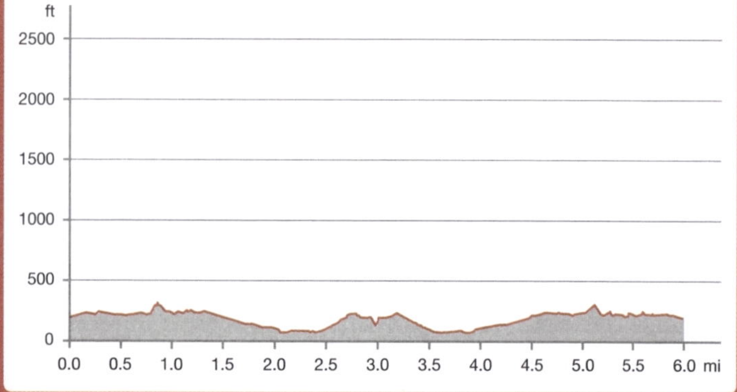

LANDS END TO BATTERY CROSBY

AN URBAN COASTAL HIKE

SAN FRANCISCO, CA

3

LENGTH
6 miles (loop)

TIME & MONEY
2 hours, free

ELEVATION GAIN
530 feet

DIFFICULTY
Moderate

CONDITIONS
Year-round; partially shaded

HIGHLIGHTS
Coastal views, urban hike

ESSENTIALS

- **Find the trailhead:** From the SoMa (South of Market) neighborhood in San Francisco, head west on Geary Street. In 2.2 miles, stay left to get on Geary Boulevard. In 3.2 miles, continue straight onto Point Lobos Avenue and proceed for 0.4 miles. The parking lot will be on the left with the Lands End Visitor Center, restrooms, and water fountains.
- **Land manager:** Golden Gate National Recreation Area (nps.gov/goga)

WHY YOU'LL LOVE IT

- Diverse landmarks in San Francisco
- Coastal views
- Dog-friendly beaches

See various San Francisco landmarks from Lands End and the iconic Baker Beach to the historic Battery Crosby, while enjoying breathtaking coastal views.

The well-marked trail starts at the opposite end of the Lands End Visitor Center, heading first to Eagle Point. Although you'll see a mix of native plant species like toyon, silver lupine, and California poppies, the dominant landscaping here includes cypress, pine, and eucalyptus trees. These non-native species were planted in the 1880s and then more heavily in the 1930s. Today, volunteers and arborists help to maintain balance of the native habitat with these non-native species.

Around 200 feet into the trail, you'll pass an optional turnoff for the historic Sutro Baths. The Sutro Baths were built in 1896 by millionaire Adolph Sutro, who originally made his fortune from entrepreneurship in silver mines. He later became a real estate developer and developed this area around Lands End. One of his developments was a massive public bathhouse that could fit up to 10,000 people among its seven swimming pools. Although the baths eventually became difficult to manage commercially and were destroyed by a fire in 1966, the ruins are open to the public to explore.

The trail continues to meander along the coast, with spectacular views of the Golden Gate Bridge. The Golden Gate Bridge was a 1.7-mile engineering marvel in the 1930s because it connects a wide bay despite regular strong winds from the ocean. At the time, the "International Orange" color was seen as a bold decision. Irving Morrow, the Golden Gate's consulting architect, advocated for the unique and unconventional color because he felt it matched the bridge's construction. "What has been thus played up in form should not be let down in color," said Morrow. Today, it's one of the world's most famous and photographed bridges.

Around two miles in, the trail cuts through a small section of residential houses before ending at Baker Beach. This mile-long beach is a famous San Francisco landmark that also happens to be dog friendly. The sand is soft and offers more dramatic views of the Golden Gate Bridge on a clear day. Heads up—at the north end of the beach, you may see clothing-optional sunbathers.

Your last stop before turning around is the historic Battery Crosby. Built in 1900, it was part of the city's military fortifications, designed to protect the entrance to San Francisco Bay. It was armed with 6-inch disappearing guns and played an important role in the San Francisco harbor's WWII history.

TURN-BY-TURN DIRECTIONS

1. From the Lands End trailhead sign, continue straight on the Coastal Trail toward the signposted "Eagles Point." After 200 feet, pass Sutro Baths on your left. Continue straight.
2. At 0.2 miles, reach the USS *SF* Memorial Viewpoint on your right. Continue straight.
3. At 0.6 miles, continue left at the marked junction toward Eagles Point. Immediately after turning left, reach the labyrinth on your left. Continue straight.
4. At 1.3 miles, turn left at the signed junction to continue on the Coastal Trail. This begins a short section on the sidewalk through residential streets.
5. At 2.0 miles, turn left onto 25th Avenue North. In 200 feet, the street ends. At this point, turn right and head down a set of stairs to re-enter the Golden Gate National Recreation Area and arrive at Baker Beach. Continue on the unmarked sand path that runs behind and parallel to the shoreline.
6. At 2.2 miles, continue straight on the signposted Coastal Trail toward the Golden Gate Bridge. After 300 feet, continue following the unmarked path left, through the parking lot and toward the Golden Gate Bridge.
7. At 2.3 miles, continue right at the sign for the Coastal Trail toward the Golden Gate Bridge.
8. At 2.5 miles, turn right at the sign for the Coastal Trail.
9. At 2.8 miles, turn left, following the sign for the Batteries to Bluffs Trail.
10. At 2.9 miles, turn left to stay on the Batteries to Bluffs Trail. In 200 feet, you'll reach Battery Crosby. When you're ready, return the way you came.

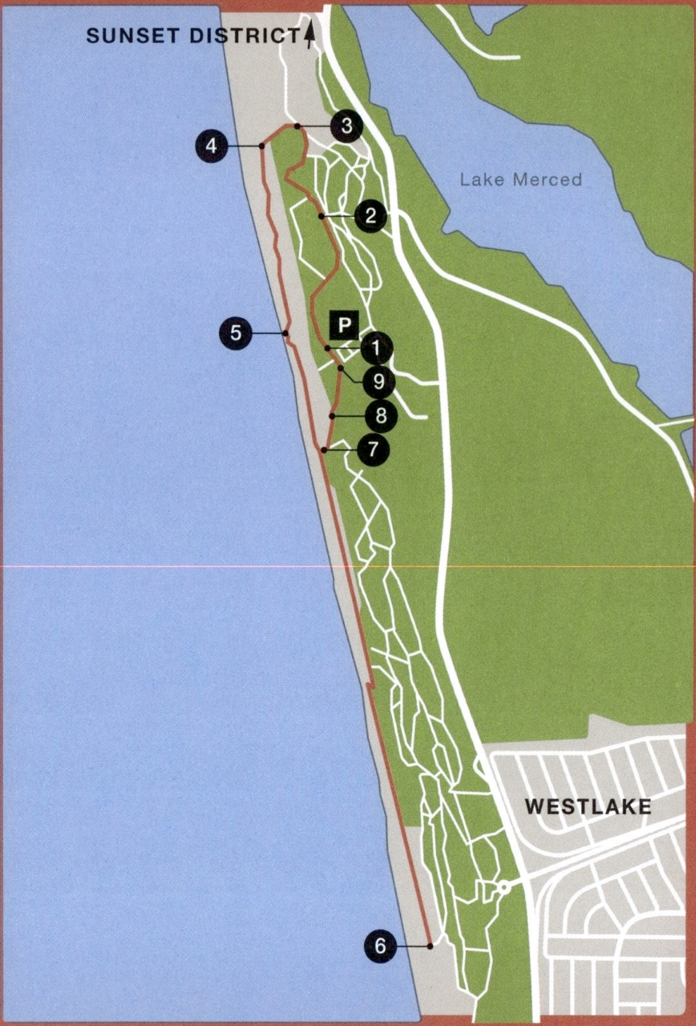

SUNSET DISTRICT
Lake Merced
WESTLAKE
P
1
2
3
4
5
6
7
8
9

P Parking

ft
2000
1500
1000
500
0
0.0
0.5
1.0
1.5
2.0
2.5
3.0
3.5
3.8
mi

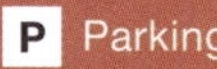

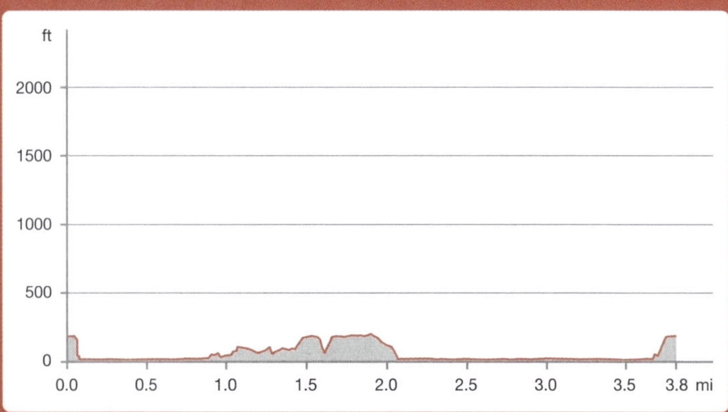

FORT FUNSTON

AN OFF-LEASH DOG BEACH BELOW HIGH BLUFFS

SAN FRANCISCO, CA

4

LENGTH
3.8 miles (loop)

TIME & MONEY
2 hours, free

ELEVATION GAIN
151 feet

DIFFICULTY
Moderate

CONDITIONS
Year-round

HIGHLIGHTS
Off-leash, beach, high bluffs

ESSENTIALS

- **Find the trailhead:** From the west side of San Francisco, take CA Route 1 southbound; proceed for 5 miles. Turn right onto Sloat Boulevard. In 1.1 miles, take a slight left onto CA-35 Skyline Boulevard. In 1.6 miles, turn right onto Fort Funston Road. Stay right until you dead-end into the parking lot, which will be in 0.2 miles.

- **Land manager:** Golden Gate National Recreation Area (nps.gov/goga).

WHY YOU'LL LOVE IT

- Dog-friendly, off-leash beaches
- Convenient location in San Francisco
- Ability to adjust the hike to be longer or shorter

Hike down steep, sandy bluffs and let your dog roam free on an off-leash beach, located in the southwest corner of San Francisco.

Fort Funston was a former military base in 1900 and home to one of the Bay Area's Nike missile defense sites during the Cold War. Today, Fort Funston is a wide stretch of sandy beaches and steep bluffs up to 200 feet high, although you may see large structures remnant from the military activity along your hike. There is a large network of hiking trails, some of which lead down to dog-friendly beaches like Funston Beach, where dogs are allowed off-leash year-round.

Starting at Sunset Trail, you'll walk along a gentle paved road and slowly descend to the ocean bluffs. The trail is lined with non-native highway iceplants, which were introduced to the area to stabilize the dunes. You'll also pass a water fountain that is a popular gathering spot for the dogs.

Once you leave the paved trail, you'll head down the sandy Funston Beach Trail. The descent is steep and footing can be tricky, so be mindful as you make your way down. Once you're down at the beach, you can look back at the dramatic cliffs that characterize Fort Funston. The famous San Andreas Fault that runs through California has helped shape many geographical landscapes, including the cliffs at Fort Funston.

When you get down to Funston Beach, your dogs will love running in the sand. The ocean waves can be unpredictable, so stay alert if your dogs decide to run into the water. This stretch of beach extends for nearly two miles, as Funston Beach becomes Phillip Burton Memorial Beach and then Thornton State Beach. When you're ready to head back, turn around and walk back the way you came. You'll reach a short but strenuous ascent back up the bluffs on the Sand Ladder Trail.

TURN-BY-TURN DIRECTIONS

1. From the parking lot, look for a trailhead kiosk and sign that marks the Sunset Trail, located at the west end of the parking lot.
2. At 0.3 miles, pass a water fountain and stay left on the Sunset Trail.
3. At 0.6 miles at the end of the paved trail, take a left onto the Funston Beach Trail.
4. At 0.7 miles, turn left onto the beach.
5. At 1.1 miles, continue past large concrete structures with graffiti on them.
6. At 2.5 miles, return the way you came along the beach.
7. At 3.6 miles, before you pass the concrete structures again, you'll see a set of stairs further ahead and up on the cliffs. There will be an opening between sand mounds on your right to an unmarked trail. Turn right at this opening, away from the beach and towards the cliffs. After 100 feet at a fork in the unmarked trail, stay left towards the direction of the stairs.
8. At 3.7 miles, head up the steep set of stairs called the Sand Ladder Trail.
9. At 3.8 miles, the trail ends at the southwest corner of the parking lot.

PACIFICA

MONTARA

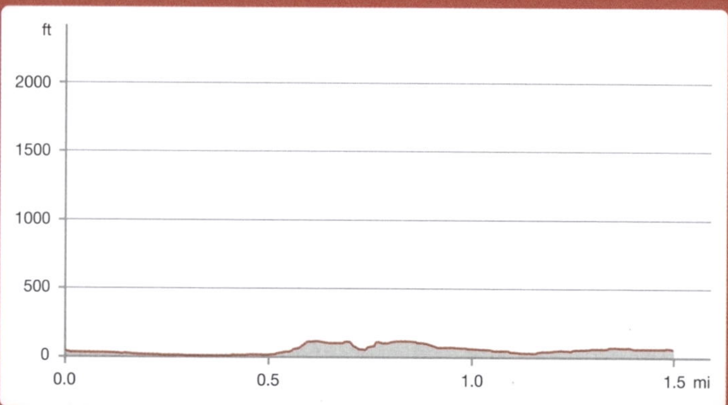

MORI POINT

SWEEPING VIEWS OF THE PACIFIC OCEAN

PACIFICA, CA

5

LENGTH
1.5 miles (loop)

TIME & MONEY
1 hour, free

ELEVATION GAIN
92 feet

DIFFICULTY
Easy

CONDITIONS
Year-round; exposed, coastal weather

HIGHLIGHTS
Ocean views, wildflowers

ESSENTIALS

- **Find the trailhead:** From San Francisco, take Interstate 280 southbound towards Daly City. After 6.5 miles, keep right at the fork to continue on CA-1 southbound towards Pacifica. After 0.2 miles, turn right onto Edgewood Road. After 5 miles, turn right onto Bradford Way. The trailhead is in 0.2 miles, at the corner where Bradford Way becomes Mori Point Road. You'll find street parking on both Bradford Way and Mori Point Road.
- **Land manager:** Golden Gate National Recreation Area (nps.gov/goga).

WHY YOU'LL LOVE IT

- Gentle hike for all types of dogs
- Optional dog-friendly beach adjacent to the trail
- Beautiful coastal views

Soak in the ocean breeze and coastal views at Mori Point. In the spring, the bluffs explode with wildflower blooms.

Mori Point is a 110-acre coastal park in Pacifica that is part of the larger Golden Gate National Recreation Area. The area is best known for dramatic coastal landscapes. On a clear day, you'll be rewarded with views as far north as to Mount Tamalpais and south to Pedro Point. Dog owners will love the gentle trail of Mori Point, which makes it easier on their dogs' paws and joints. Dogs on leash are also allowed on the adjacent Sharp Park State Beach.

In the spring, Mori Point is well known for its wildflower display. The amount of spring flowers will vary, based on factors such as recent rain and temperatures. The most common wildflower species in Mori Point are goldfields, tidy tips, checkerblooms, and poppies, the official state flower of California.

After leaving the trailhead, you'll walk along a boardwalk with interpretive signs explaining the history of Mori Point. At the roundabout, you'll see Sharp Park Beach just beyond the trail. However, to get to Mori Point, you'll instead take a left and go up a short set of stairs called Bootlegger's Steps. The steps were named after "rumrunners" who used to bring illegal liquor to supply the speakeasy at the Mori Inn and restaurant during Prohibition. Once you reach the top of the stairs, you'll only need to hike a few hundred feet more to get to Mori Point. If you're lucky, you may be able to catch a glimpse of marine mammals along the coast; winter and spring are typically the best time to see humpback and blue whales. Binoculars can be helpful too.

Your hike back to the trailhead takes you down through the Lishumsha Trail. "Lishumsha" is the Ohlone word for garter snake. The Ohlone are Indigenous people of the San Francisco Bay Area who continue to have an important impact on Bay Area communities. Unfortunately, the San Francisco garter snake has been an endangered species since 1967 due to habitat loss and change, illegal collection, and the decline of a key food source, the California red-legged frog. The San Francisco garter snake still inhabits Mori Point, where staff and volunteers help support the species through their restoration efforts.

TURN-BY-TURN DIRECTIONS

1. From the trailhead kiosk, follow a dirt path on Old Mori Road.
2. At 0.2 miles, continue on the wooden boardwalk.
3. At 0.3 miles, pass the interpretive signs about the history of Mori Point.
4. At 0.4 miles, take a left around the roundabout. You'll see Sharp Park Beach (unmarked) on your right and a set of wooden stairs called Bootlegger's Steps (unmarked) straight ahead of you.
5. At 0.6 miles, pass a wooden bench halfway up Bootlegger's Steps. After 100 feet, you'll reach the top of the stairs, which is at the intersection of multiple trails. Take an immediate right onto the Mori Headlands Trail.
6. At 0.7 miles, reach Mori Point. After enjoying the view, return to the top of Bootlegger's Steps.
7. At 0.8 miles, back at the top of Bootlegger's Steps, take a slight left at the intersection of multiple trails, onto the marked Coastal Trail towards the Lishumsha Trail.
8. At 1.0 miles, continue straight onto the Lishumsha Trail.
9. At 1.1 miles, take a slight right onto the Upper Mori Trail.
10. At 1.5 miles, turn left to head back to the trailhead start.

SAN PABLO

ORINDA

SAN PABLO

ALBANY

Parking Toilet Bench Picnic table

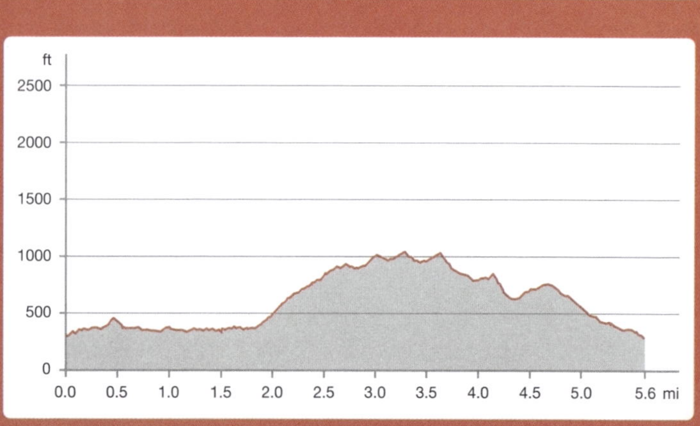

WILDCAT CANYON REGIONAL PARK

PASTORAL VIEWS OF ROLLING HILLS

RICHMOND, CA

6

LENGTH

5.6 miles (lollipop loop)

TIME & MONEY

2 hours 15 min., free

ELEVATION GAIN

761 feet

DIFFICULTY

Moderate

CONDITIONS

Year-round; mostly exposed

HIGHLIGHTS

Grazing cattle, panoramic vistas, off-leash sections

ESSENTIALS

- **Find the trailhead:** From downtown Oakland, take Interstate 980 east. In 0.6 miles, merge onto Interstate 580 west toward San Francisco. In 1.5 miles, merge onto Interstate 580 west/Interstate 80 east toward Berkeley/Sacramento. In 8.6 miles, take the exit for Solano Avenue. In 0.1 miles, merge left onto Amador Street and continue for 0.4 miles. Turn right onto McBryde Avenue. In 0.2 miles, continue straight to stay on McBryde Avenue, which becomes Park Avenue in 100 feet. In 0.2 miles, turn left onto Wildcat Canyon Parkway to reach the parking lot, where there are dog waste bags but no trash bins or water source. The trailhead is at the very end of the parking lot.
- **Land manager:** East Bay Regional Park District (ebparks.org)

WHY YOU'LL LOVE IT

- Hike alongside cattle
- Panoramic vistas of the Bay Area
- Off-leash trail sections
- Historical ruins of a sanitarium

Hike near cattle grazing at Wildcat Canyon Regional Park. While traversing the ridgelines and hills, enjoy stunning views of the San Francisco Bay.

Wildcat Canyon Regional Park sits in the East Bay hills and connects to other dog-friendly East Bay regional parks such as Tilden Regional Park (see the Tilden Regional Park chapter). Wildcat Canyon has over 2,700 acres of rolling grasslands and ridgeline trails that provide some of the best panoramic views in the East Bay.

You'll start the hike on the wide Wildcat Creek Trail, where dogs can be off-leash for about two miles. The trail begins as a paved path for the first half-mile, passing a variety of plant species, such as the invasive French broom. With its bright-yellow springtime flowers, French broom is effective at controlling erosion but is notorious for crowding out native plants.

As you continue into the park for the next mile and a half, the trail surface will change to gravel and dirt. You'll walk through a brief shaded area before arriving at a cattle gate. Leash your dogs before you open the cattle gate and ensure that the gate is closed completely behind you. As soon as you pass through the gate, it's possible to see cattle year-round and calves from August to October. The East Bay Regional Park District manages the grazing program to keep the grasslands healthy and mitigate wildfire risk. Be sure to give the cattle space—while they are generally indifferent and ignore humans and dogs, interacting with cattle can be dangerous to both the animals and yourself.

Over the next mile, you'll climb several hundred feet as you hike up the rolling hills, which are particularly stunning in the spring, when they're green from the winter's rain. With the pastoral scene of green hills and grazing cattle, it's easy to forget you're just minutes from a major metropolitan area. The hills begin turning brown in summer, though the timing varies with the year's rainfall. Around three miles in, you'll reach the San Pablo Ridge Trail, where you'll have unobstructed views of the San Francisco Bay for the next mile.

As you turn onto the Belgum Trail, you'll begin a steeper descent back down the hill. You may continue to see cattle on both the San Pablo Ridge Trail and the Belgum Trail. At the end of the hike, you'll see several palm trees that seem completely out of place in relation to the grasslands. These trees were part of the Grande Vista Sanitarium that operated from the early 1900s until 1963. In 1977, vandals burned the estate, and the only remnants of the sanitarium are the palm trees and a small stone wall.

TURN-BY-TURN DIRECTIONS

1. From the trailhead, head straight onto the paved Wildcat Creek Trail.
2. At 0.3 miles, continue straight at the marked junction to start the loop counter-clockwise.
3. At 1.8 miles, there's a picnic table and trash can on your right. Turn left at the marked junction onto the Mezue Trail. Leash your dogs before walking through the cattle gate.
4. At 2.7 miles, continue straight at the marked junction to stay on the Mezue Trail.
5. At 2.9 miles, continue straight again at the marked junction to stay on the Mezue Trail.
6. At 3.1 miles, turn left at the marked junction onto the San Pablo Ridge Trail.
7. At 4.3 miles, continue straight at the marked junction onto the Belgum Trail.
8. At 4.5 miles, continue straight at the marked junction to stay on the Belgum Trail.
9. At 4.7 miles, continue straight again at the marked junction to stay on the Belgum Trail.
10. At 4.9 miles, there will be several unmarked, narrow side trails. Ignore all of them and continue on the Belgum Trail.
11. At 5.2 miles, arrive at a sign with information about the Grande Vista Sanitarium. When you're ready, continue straight on the Belgum Trail.
12. At 5.3 miles, continue straight through the cattle gate. After 400 feet, complete the loop and arrive back at Step 2. Turn right to retrace your steps back to the parking lot.

10
11
P
1
2
3
9
8
7
ORINDA
BERKELEY
4
5
6

P Parking | Picnic area | Bench | Viewpoint

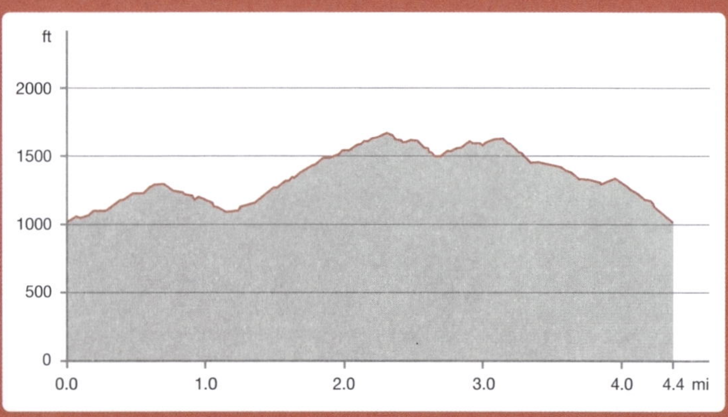

TILDEN REGIONAL PARK

OFF-LEASH HIKE WITH PANORAMIC VISTAS

BERKELEY, CA

7

LENGTH
4.4 miles (loop)

TIME & MONEY
2 hours 15 min., free

ELEVATION GAIN
980 feet

DIFFICULTY
Moderate

CONDITIONS
Year-round; exposed, sunny

HIGHLIGHTS
Panoramic vistas, off-leash

ESSENTIALS

- **Find the trailhead:** From Downtown Oakland, take CA-24 East. In 4.4 miles, turn slightly right to stay on CA-24 East (signs for California 24). In 0.9 miles, take the exit for Fish Ranch Road. In 0.3 miles, turn right onto Fish Ranch Road. In 0.8 miles, turn right onto Grizzly Peak Boulevard. In 3 miles, turn right onto Golf Course Drive. In 0.9 miles, turn right onto Shasta Road. In 0.3 miles, turn right onto Wildcat Canyon Road. In 1.0 miles, the parking lot will be on your right.

- **Land manager:** East Bay Regional Park District (ebparks.org)

WHY YOU'LL LOVE IT

- Panoramic vistas of the Bay Area
- Off-leash trails
- Picnic area at the trailhead

Enjoy off-leash hiking with your pup as you loop around Tilden Regional Park and soak in views of the San Francisco Bay and San Pablo Dam Reservoir.

Tilden Regional Park sits in the Berkeley hills and connects to other dog-friendly East Bay parks such as Wildcat Canyon Regional Park (see the Wildcat Canyon Regional Park chapter). Sitting at just over 2,000 acres, Tilden Regional Park offers attractions such as a steam train, a botanic garden, and a farm with sheep, goats, and other animals. Most of its 39 miles of hiking trails are dog-friendly, with many of the hikes permitting off-leash dogs.

To begin your hike, you'll cross the Quarry Picnic Area, where you can enjoy a snack with your pups at the picnic tables. There are limited facilities available here, so you'll need to pack your own water. The first half mile is partially exposed on a dirt trail, taking you up the hillside. After you've transitioned from the Quarry Trail to the Lower Big Springs Trail, you'll reach sweeping views of the San Francisco Bay, the city skyline, and Marin. Looking closer at the San Francisco skyline, you'll see a few prominent buildings, including the 1,070-foot-tall Salesforce Tower and 853-foot-tall Transamerica Pyramid.

San Francisco's history of skyscrapers reflects the history of institutions in power, urban development, and architectural achievement. In 1890, the first skyscraper in San Francisco, standing at 218 feet, was built by Michael H. de Young, co-founder of the *San Francisco Chronicle* newspaper.

Five years later in 1895, Claus Spreckels bought a rival newspaper, *The San Francisco Call*, and commissioned the Call Building, which was to be 97 feet taller than the Chronicle Building.

Today, the tallest skyscraper in San Francisco is the Salesforce Tower, which was completed in 2018. Aside from being the tallest skyscraper, you can also distinguish the Salesforce Tower from its tapered cylindrical shape and rounded corners—architectural design choices specific to this modern era.

Once on the Upper Big Springs Trail, you'll start a steep ascent up 600 feet over the next mile as you hike from the Upper Big Springs Trail onto the Seaview Trail. As you climb, you'll be rewarded with additional views of San Francisco and the San Pablo Dam Reservoir.

The San Pablo Dam Reservoir is a man-made reservoir owned by the East Bay Municipal Utility District (often called East Bay MUD). The water comes from a couple of hundred miles away in the Mokelumne River watershed in the Sierra Nevada and is moved via aqueducts to the San Pablo Dam Reservoir. Although it may only supply around 10 percent of the East Bay district's total water supply, it's an important reservoir for the overall water-management system, especially in high drought years.

Around three miles in, you'll reach a labyrinth that hikers have built and maintained over time. While it's not an official viewpoint, it serves as a good meditative or resting point on the hike. After the labyrinth, you'll begin your descent for the next mile back to the parking lot, completing the loop.

TURN-BY-TURN DIRECTIONS

1. From the trailhead, head onto the Quarry Trail. After 350 feet, stay right at the signpost to continue on the Quarry Trail.
2. At 0.4 miles, take a slight left at the signpost to get on the Lower Big Springs Trail.
3. At 0.5 miles, reach a view of San Francisco to your right.
4. At 1.2 miles, leash your dogs at the signpost. Continue straight through the parking lot and then onto the Upper Big Springs Trail.
5. At 1.9 miles, turn right onto the signposted Seaview Trail.
6. At 2.2 miles, you'll see another viewpoint of the San Francisco Bay to your right. Turn left at the unmarked junction to make a U-Turn onto the Fenceline Trail.
7. At 2.4 miles, continue straight at the unmarked junction to continue on the Fenceline Trail.
8. At 2.7 miles, turn right at the signposted junction onto the Seaview Trail.
9. At 3.1 miles, reach a rock circle and a bench on your left with more views of San Francisco.
10. At 4.0 miles, continue straight to stay on the signposted Seaview Trail.
11. At 4.2 miles, continue straight at the signposted junction to head back toward the Quarry Picnic Area and to the parking lot, where there is a trash bin and portable toilet.

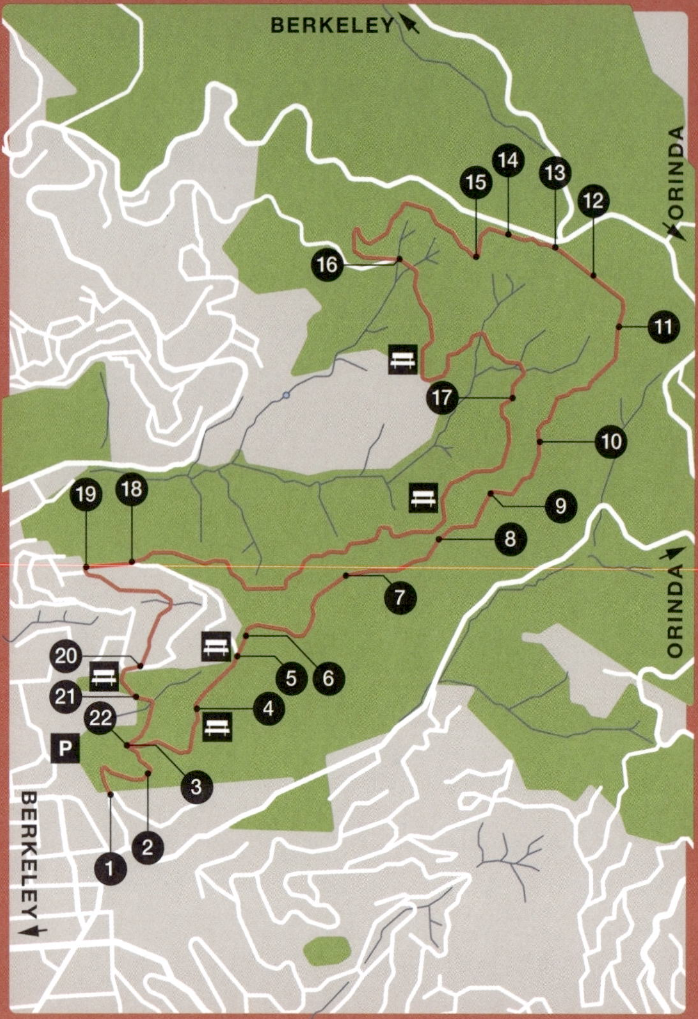

BERKELEY

ORINDA

ORINDA

BERKELEY

P Parking

Bench

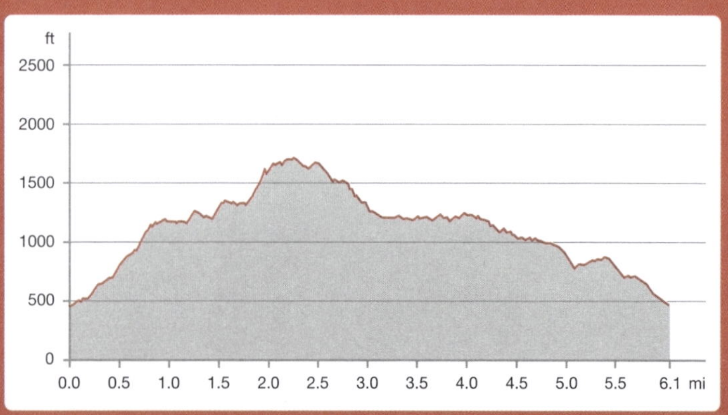

CLAREMONT CANYON AND UC BERKELEY

OFF-LEASH RIDGE CLIMB WITH VARIED VIEWS

BERKELEY, CA

LENGTH
6.1 miles (lollipop loop)

TIME & MONEY
3 hours 15 min., free

ELEVATION GAIN
1,236 feet

DIFFICULTY
Strenuous

CONDITIONS
Year-round; mostly exposed

HIGHLIGHTS
Panoramic vistas, off-leash trails

ESSENTIALS

- **Find the trailhead:** From downtown Oakland, take CA-24 east. In 1.6 miles, take the exit for Claremont Avenue. In 0.2 miles, turn left onto Claremont Avenue. In 1.6 miles, turn left onto Stonewall Road. In 0.1 miles, the trailhead and a trash bin for dog waste are on your left. Street parking is available on surrounding streets but may have a 2-hour restriction on weekdays. Non-restrictive parking is available south of Claremont Avenue and Ashby Avenue.
- **Land manager:** East Bay Regional Park District (ebparks.org) and UC Berkeley (berkeley.edu)

WHY YOU'LL LOVE IT

- Panoramic vistas of the Bay Area
- Off-leash trails
- Steep but rewarding climbs

Enjoy off-leash climbs through eucalyptus groves and oak forests. You'll enjoy spectacular vistas of the bay, San Francisco, and the rolling Berkeley Hills.

Your hike begins in the Claremont Canyon Regional Preserve. In the mid-1800s, Claremont Canyon was known as Telegraph Canyon because a transcontinental telegraph line ran through the area. Horses and wagons relied on the canyon to travel between Oakland and Contra Costa County in the northeast. Even Pony Express riders used this route to carry mail.

The first half mile climbs through towering eucalyptus trees before opening up to views of the San Francisco Bay. In the late 1800s and early 1900s, people believed eucalyptus trees were excellent for lumber, so they planted this non-native species all over California, including in Claremont Canyon. Unfortunately, we've since discovered that eucalyptus are both damaging to native biodiversity and very flammable, making it an especially problematic invasive species in this fire-prone environment.

At the top of the ridge, the landscape changes to a mix of redwoods, shrubs, and grassland. In the spring and early summer, look out for the yellow flowers of the native golden yarrow. Around two miles in, you'll arrive at a wooden arch-like structure next to a cherry plum tree. The structure provides great framing for the view of the bay, San Francisco, and Marin.

When you turn onto the Upper Jordan Fire Trail about three miles into the hike, you'll enjoy a nice view into the canyon. In the 1970s, UC Berkeley attempted to remove the eucalyptus trees in this area, and the Piedmont Rotary Club helped plant redwood trees in their place. However, the felled eucalyptus grew back and continue to compete with redwoods for resources. The Claremont Canyon Conservancy continues UC Berkeley's work to replace fire-hazard eucalyptus with fire-safe species like redwoods and oaks.

Around mile five, you'll reach a short connector trail with loose gravel—this can be a bit slippery coming down, so be careful. After a brief stint on a paved road in a quiet neighborhood, you'll take the Clark Kerr Trail to reconnect with the initial half-mile climb and head back down to the trailhead.

TURN-BY-TURN DIRECTIONS

1. From the trailhead, pass the gate to start on the Stonewall-Claremont Trail. Your dog can be off-leash starting at this point. After 500 feet, continue straight to stay on the trail, ignoring the trail on the left at the arrow sign.
2. At 0.2 miles, keep left, ignoring the unmarked trail on the right.
3. At 0.4 miles, continue on the main trail, which curves right, ignoring the unmarked trail on the left. This marks the start of the loop.
4. At 0.6 miles, start a steep ascent with loose rock.
5. At 0.8 miles, walk past the gate and turn right onto the unmarked paved road. After 300 feet, reach an unmarked dirt path for the East West Trail.
6. At 0.9 miles, keep right at the unmarked fork to continue on the trail.
7. At 1.1 miles, continue straight at the unmarked junction, up a steep ascent.
8. At 1.3 miles, continue straight at the unmarked junction.
9. At 1.5 miles, continue on the trail straight ahead, ignoring the small unmarked trail branching out left.
10. At 1.7 miles, continue straight at the unmarked four-way junction. After 200 feet, keep left at the unmarked junction.
11. At 2.0 miles, reach a wooden arch-like structure on your left. Continue straight at the unmarked junction. After 100 feet, continue straight again at the unmarked junction.
12. At 2.2 miles, continue straight at the unmarked junction.
13. At 2.3 miles, continue on a narrow connector trail running parallel to the road. Don't cross the road.
14. At 2.4 miles, stay right to continue on the trail parallel to the road. After 500 feet, the connector trail becomes the Convict Trail (unmarked), which goes back into the canyon and away from the road.
15. At 2.5 miles, stay right at the unmarked junction to continue on the Convict Trail.
16. At 3.0 miles, turn left at the unmarked junction onto the Upper Jordan Fire Trail.
17. At 3.7 miles, stay right at the unmarked fork.
18. At 4.9 miles, turn right onto a connector trail for the Lower Jordan Trail. Signage is posted on a call box at the junction. If your dog is off-leash, leash them here before the road ahead.
19. At 5.0 miles at the bottom of the hill, turn left and then take another immediate left to turn onto Panoramic Way (a paved road).
20. At 5.4 miles, turn right at the T-junction. After 200 feet, before you reach the road signs, turn left onto the unmarked Clark Kerr Trail and take a set of wooden stairs down 200 feet.
21. At 5.6 miles, turn left at the unmarked junction to continue on the Clark Kerr Trail.
22. At 5.7 miles, reach the end of the loop from Step 3. Turn right at the unmarked junction to retrace your steps back to the trailhead.

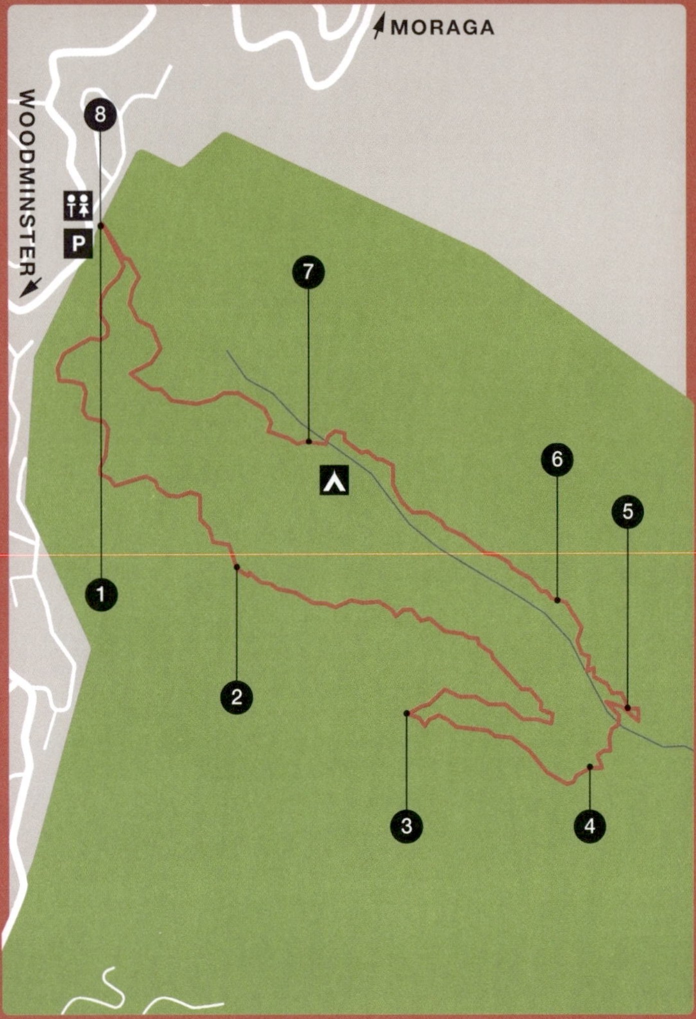

MORAGA
WOODMINSTER
8
7
6
5
1
2
3
4

P Parking · Toilet · Campground

ft
2000
1500
1000
500
0
0.0
0.5
1.0
1.5
2.0
2.5
2.7 mi

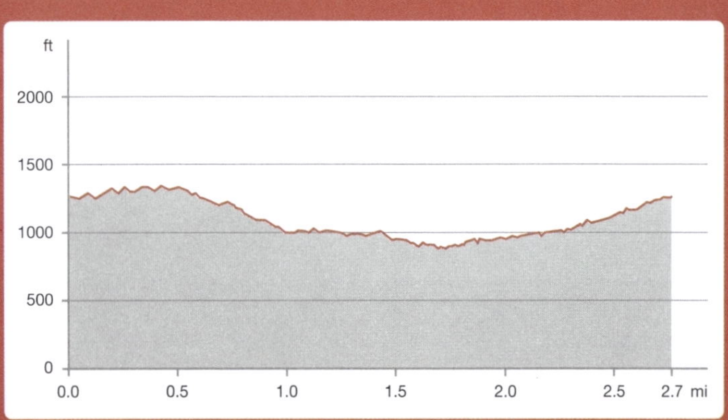

REINHARDT REDWOOD REGIONAL PARK

A REDWOOD FOREST NEAR DOWNTOWN OAKLAND

OAKLAND, CA

9

LENGTH

2.7 miles (loop)

TIME & MONEY

1 hour 15 min., free

ELEVATION GAIN

434 feet

DIFFICULTY

Easy

CONDITIONS

Year-round; partially shaded

HIGHLIGHTS

Redwood trees, off-leash areas

ESSENTIALS

- **Find the trailhead:** From Downtown Oakland, take CA-24 East. In 3.4 miles, take the exit to merge onto CA-13 South toward Hayward. In 2.4 miles, take the exit for Park Boulevard. In 0.1 miles, merge onto Trafalgar Place and stay left in 200 feet to stay on Trafalgar Place. In 50 feet, turn left at the first cross street onto Park Boulevard. In 489 feet, turn left onto Mountain Boulevard. In 0.2 miles, turn right onto Snake Road. In 0.2 miles, continue straight onto Shepherd Canyon Road. In 1.6 miles, take a sharp right to stay on Shepherd Canyon Road. In 0.2 miles, turn right onto Skyline Boulevard. The parking lot will be on your left in 0.4 miles.
- **Land manager:** East Bay Regional Parks District (ebparks.org)

WHY YOU'LL LOVE IT

- Easy access from the city to redwood trees
- Off-leash section on the hike
- Gentle footing will be accessible for most dogs

Just miles from Downtown Oakland, immerse yourself in a second- and third-generation redwood forest at Reinhardt Redwood Regional Park.

Reinhardt Redwood Regional Park is part of the dog-friendly collection of parks managed by the East Bay Regional Parks District. In 2019, the park was renamed in honor of an important Bay Area figure, Dr. Aurelia Henry Reinhardt. Born in San Francisco, she was president of Mills College in Oakland from 1916 to 1943 and played an important role in the formation of the East Bay Regional Park District in 1934. Aurelia was an early advocate for protecting the redwoods in California and was influential in providing open space opportunities for the public.

This hike aligns with Aurelia's vision to create accessible open spaces, as the trailhead is only a few miles away from downtown Oakland and the hike's gentle terrain makes it accessible for most dogs and their owners. This hike brings the beauty of redwoods to the East Bay's backyard.

As soon as you get on the West Ridge Trail about 200 feet into your hike, you'll be able to take your dog off-leash for the next mile and a half. The West Ridge Trail starts with a flat approach past various tree species like California bay laurels and eucalyptus. The California bay laurel is a native evergreen tree that thrives in moist and shaded areas alongside redwood trees, with dark-green and elongated leaves.

Half a mile into the hike, you'll begin a gentle descent on the French and Tres Sendas Trails, where you'll start to see more concentrated redwood trees. Most of the coastal redwoods here are second-growth, as they recovered from extensive logging in the 1800s. While some of the redwood trees at Reinhardt Redwood Regional Park are up to 150 feet tall, shorter plant species line the forest floor. Western sword fern, pacific trillium, and western starflower grow beneath the canopy and are a critical part of a healthy forest ecosystem. Tall coastal redwoods allow only small amounts of sunlight to come through, creating a cool and moist environment for the understory plants. These forest plants then provide food, shelter, and protection for birds, insects, and small mammals, while also providing important structure and nutrients for the surrounding soil.

When you turn onto the Steam Trail toward the end of the loop, you'll need to re-leash your dog. Redwood Creek runs through the Steam Trail and is an important part of the sensitive habitat. Rainbow trout and California newt are primary inhabitants of Redwood Creek, and they need high water quality in order to reproduce and thrive. Keeping your dogs on the trails and out of the creek will help keep the sensitive species healthy.

As you make your way back to the parking lot, you'll pass Girl's Camp. Girl's Camp is a primitive group campsite that campers can reserve in the summer. It's a dog-friendly camp, which makes it a great camping option if you intend to explore for longer.

TURN-BY-TURN DIRECTIONS

1. At the trailhead, head right at the sign for the West Ridge Trail. Once you pass the sign around 200 feet further, dogs may be off-leash.
2. At 0.6 miles, turn left onto the signposted French Trail.
3. At 1.2 miles, turn left onto the signposted Tres Sendas Trail.
4. At 1.5 miles, turn left at the sign to stay on the Tres Sendas Trail.
5. At 1.6 miles, turn left onto the signposted Stream Trail. Dogs need to be leashed from this point on.
6. At 1.9 miles, continue straight on the signposted Stream Trail.
7. At 2.2 miles, pass Girl's Camp campground on your left. Continue straight on the Stream Trail.
8. At 2.7 miles, arrive back at the trailhead, where there are water fountains, trash receptacles, and restrooms.

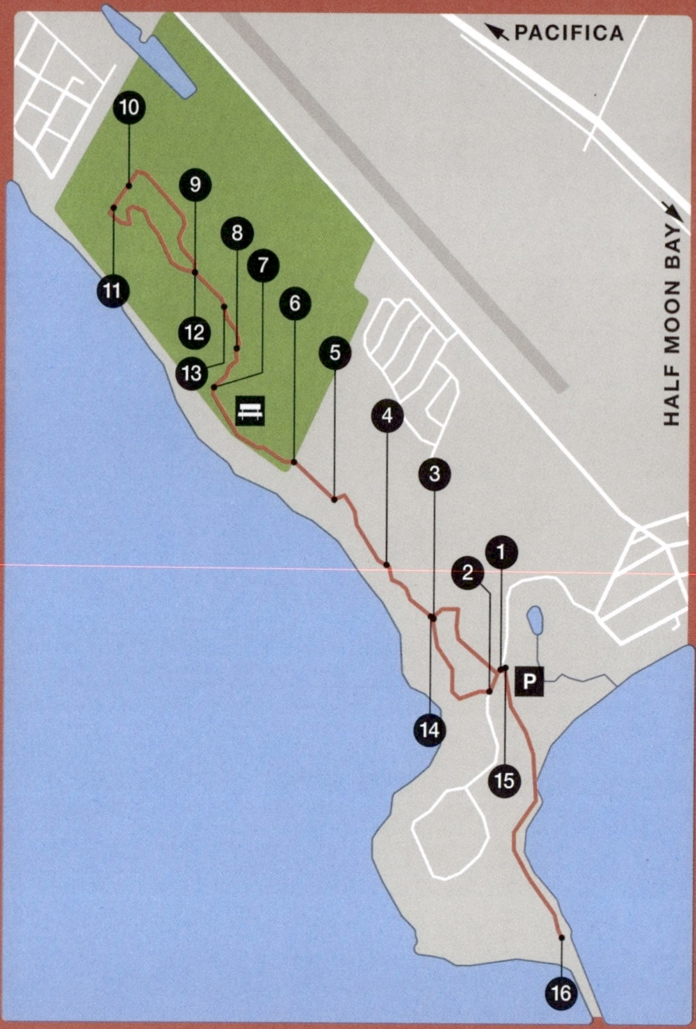

PACIFICA
HALF MOON BAY
1
2
3
4
5
6
7
8
9
10
11
12
13
14
15
16
P

P Parking
Bench

ft
2500
2000
1500
1000
500
0
0.0
0.5
1.0
1.5
2.0
2.5
3.0
3.4 mi

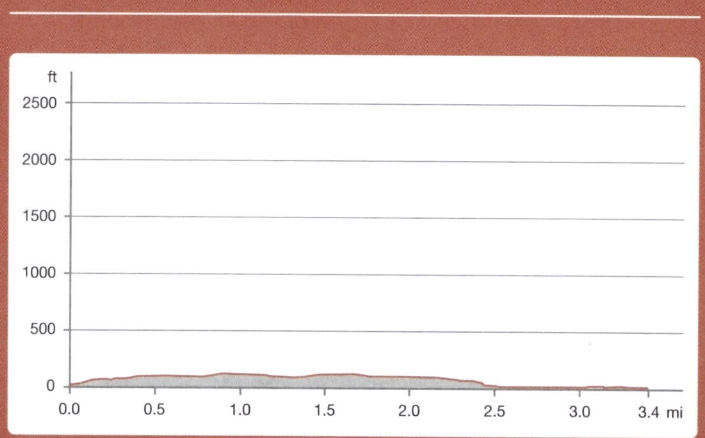

PILLAR POINT BLUFF AND MAVERICKS BEACH

BREATHTAKING BLUFFS ALONG THE OCEAN

HALF MOON BAY, CA

10

LENGTH

3.4 miles (lollipop loop)

TIME & MONEY

1 hour 30 min., free

ELEVATION GAIN

154 feet

DIFFICULTY

Easy

CONDITIONS

Year-round; exposed, coastal weather

HIGHLIGHTS

Coastal views, dog-friendly beach

ESSENTIALS

- **Find the trailhead:** From Palo Alto, take Interstate 280 northbound. After 11 miles, take the exit for CA-92 West toward Half Moon Bay. At the intersection with CA-35 in 2.3 miles, continue straight to follow CA-92 West. In 5.1 miles, turn right onto CA-1 North. After 3.7 miles, turn left onto Capistrano Road. In 0.4 miles, turn left onto Prospect Way. Take the first right onto Broadway after 350 feet and then your first left onto Harvard Avenue in 95 feet. In 0.4 miles, reach the end of Harvard Avenue and turn right onto W Point Avenue. Continue on W Point Avenue for 0.4 miles until you reach a large gravel parking lot on your left, marked by a blue sign prohibiting vehicles between sunset and sunrise.
- **Land manager:** San Mateo County Parks Department (smcgov.org/parks)

WHY YOU'LL LOVE IT

- Moderate temperatures for comfortable hiking
- Gentle terrain for your dog's paws
- Option to cool off in the ocean at Mavericks Beach

Hike gentle trails on Pillar Point Bluff with views of the Pacific Ocean the entire way. Enjoy an option to cool off at Mavericks Beach at the end of the hike.

Pillar Point Bluff is a 220-acre bluff that sits high atop the Pacific Ocean and offers views of the surrounding area, including Half Moon Bay, Pillar Point Harbor, and the Pillar Point Air Force Station. The temperatures are moderate year-round, and the trail is gentle in elevation, with only 154 feet across one mile to get you to the top of the bluff. Both of these characteristics make Pillar Point Bluff a great option for dogs of all ages and athletic abilities.

You'll start your hike on Ross's Cove Trail, across the street from the Pillar Point Marsh parking lot, which'll take you to the top of Pillar Point Bluff. From the start, you'll immediately see a white structure that resembles a giant golf ball, sitting atop the bluff. This is the Pillar Point Air Force Station, a private site that supports missile launches and aeronautical testing.

During the first mile, you'll pass a Monterey cypress tree and different species of plants like California sagebrush, coffeeberry, and monkey flower. The Monterey cypress grows with distinctive branches and a dense canopy, both shaped by persistent winds and coastal conditions. After around a mile, you'll head inland on the Jean Lauer Trail, which takes you to the northern end of Pillar Point Bluff. Jean Lauer was a staffer at the Peninsula Open Space Trust, a nonprofit working to protect open space on the Peninsula and in the South Bay. You'll then head onto the Frenchman's Reef Trail, turning south to connect back to the Ross's Cove Trail.

Once you reach the parking lot, you can continue straight to the end of the lot, where there are dog waste bags and trash cans. Continue straight until you reach Mavericks Beach, where you can let your dog cool off, as dogs are allowed on-leash on the beach. Mavericks Beach is famous for having some of the biggest surf on the West Coast in the winter months. Surfers from around the world will come to Mavericks Beach when the coastal weather patterns set up big-wave conditions. In fact, there was a big-wave surf contest that was held at Mavericks Beach every year from 1999 until 2019.

TURN-BY-TURN DIRECTIONS

1. From the Pillar Point Marsh parking lot, cross the street and walk 400 feet west along the road.
2. At 400 feet, turn right onto an unmarked dirt path. In 150 feet, turn right onto the unmarked Ross's Cove Trail.
3. At 0.2 miles, continue straight on the Ross's Cove Trail.
4. At 0.4 miles, continue straight on the Ross's Cove Trail.
5. At 0.5 miles, stay left on the Ross's Cove Trail.
6. At 0.6 miles, stay left at the unmarked junction on the Ross's Cove Trail.
7. At 0.8 miles, follow the Ross's Cove Trail to the right.
8. At 0.9 miles, stay left at the unmarked junction on the Ross's Cove Trail. After 500 feet, turn left onto the signposted Jean Lauer Trail.
9. At 1.0 miles, stay right on the Jean Lauer Trail.
10. At 1.2 miles, continue straight at the unmarked junction on the Jean Lauer Trail.
11. At 1.3 miles, continue straight at the unmarked junction on the Jean Lauer Trail. In 100 feet, turn left onto the signposted Frenchman's Reef Trail.
12. At 1.5 miles, the Frenchman's Reef Trail ends and becomes the Jean Lauer Trail. Continue straight.
13. At 1.6 miles, stay right to go on the signposted Ross's Cove Trail back toward the parking lot.
14. At 2.3 miles, take a left at the unmarked junction on a dirt path toward the parking lot. In 400 feet, turn right on an unmarked paved road.
15. At 2.5 miles, arrive at the parking lot. Continue to the end of the parking lot, where you'll see a path that leads to Mavericks Beach.
16. At 3.0 miles, from Mavericks Beach, return the way you came back to the parking lot.

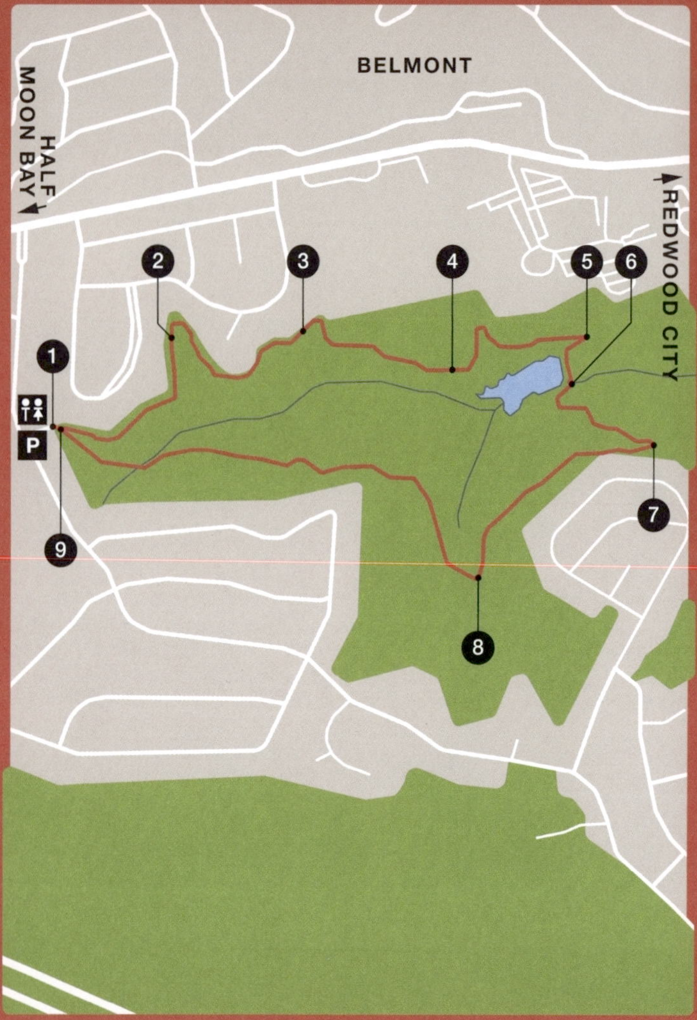

BELMONT
HALF MOON BAY
REDWOOD CITY
1
2
3
4
5
6
7
8
9
P

P Parking
Toilet

ft
2000
1500
1000
500
0
0.0
0.5
1.0
1.5
2.0 mi

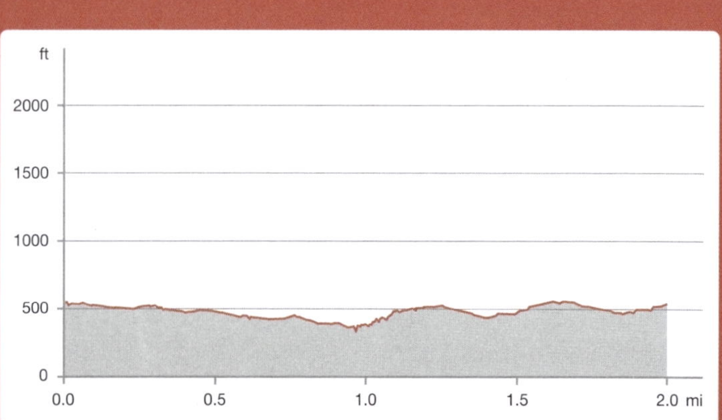

WATERDOG LAKE AND OPEN SPACE

NEIGHBORHOOD OPEN SPACE WITH QUAINT LAKE VIEWS

BELMONT, CA

11

LENGTH
2 miles (loop)

TIME & MONEY
1 hour, free

ELEVATION GAIN
220 feet

DIFFICULTY
Easy

CONDITIONS
Year-round; partially shaded

HIGHLIGHTS
Lake views

ESSENTIALS

- **Find the trailhead:** From San Mateo, follow CA-92 West towards Half Moon Bay. In 2.4 miles, take the exit for Ralston Avenue. In 0.2 miles, turn left onto Ralston Avenue. In 0.7 miles, turn right onto Hallmark Drive. In 0.2 miles, turn left on Lake Road, which dead-ends straight ahead in a couple hundred feet. Parking is on the street on either side of Lake Road. You'll find the trailhead kiosk just beyond the metal gate.

- **Land manager:** Belmont Parks and Recreation Office (https://www.belmont.gov/)

WHY YOU'LL LOVE IT

- Charming lake views
- Historic dam
- Gentle footing will be accessible for most dogs

Wander around Waterdog Lake and Open Space to enjoy quiet trails and lake views. This Bay Area neighborhood gem provides a quick escape from the urban hustle and bustle.

Waterdog Lake is a charming canyon tucked into the residential area of Belmont. The area was originally named after a local salamander species: the waterdog. Although the salamanders no longer inhabit the lake, Waterdog Lake offers both dog-friendly hiking and mountain biking trail options of varying lengths and difficulty. The trail system is best known for the small lake that sits in the northwest corner of the open space.

The parking area for Lake Road Trailhead is a residential road that dead-ends into the Lake Road Trailhead. Street parking here is available for a handful of cars, and you can find additional parking along the surrounding neighborhood streets. Lake Road Trail is a wide dirt trail that leads you to Waterdog Lake. A variety of local plant and tree species like coast live oak and toyon provide occasional shade along the trail. You may also notice staircases coming down from behind the local homes—these are private residences, and hikers should not go up to them. The first half mile has a gentle decline, taking you further into the open space and closer to the lake.

Around three fourths of a mile in, you'll reach the Lake Loop Trail, where you'll enjoy peaceful views of the small lake. Although it's called a lake, Waterdog is perhaps more similar to a reservoir because financier William Ralston created it with a dam in the late 1800s to supply water to his estate. As you cross a small bridge to continue onto the Berry Trail, you'll spot remnants of the dam on your left.

After leaving the lake, you'll finish your hike by climbing back up via the John Brooks Trail. The John Brooks Trail is a wide, dirt trail with reduced vegetation that connects the west and east sections of the open space. After the trail opens up, it remains unshaded for the remainder of the hike as you loop back to the parking area.

TURN-BY-TURN DIRECTIONS

1. From the trailhead kiosk, bear left to follow the Lake Road Trail.
2. At 0.3 miles, follow the trail right to stay on the unmarked Lake Road Trail and avoid the stairs up to local residences.
3. At 0.5 miles, bear right again to stay on the unmarked Lake Road Trail and avoid the stairs up to local residences.
4. At 0.7 miles, keep right once more to stay on the Lake Road Trail and avoid the stairs up to local residences.
5. At 0.9 miles, take a sharp right to proceed on the Lake Loop Trail. After 300 feet, turn left, crossing a small wooden bridge.
6. At 1.0 miles, turn left onto the Berry Trail. After 150 feet, continue across a wooden ramp.
7. At 1.2 miles, turn right onto the connector for the John Brooks Trail. In 100 feet, turn right onto the John Brooks Trail to loop back toward the parking area.
8. At 1.4 miles, continue right on the John Brooks Trail. Continue straight for the next 0.6 miles, ignoring two unmarked trail spurs on the right.
9. At 2.0 miles, turn left onto the paved road. The parking area and trailhead is 100 feet ahead.

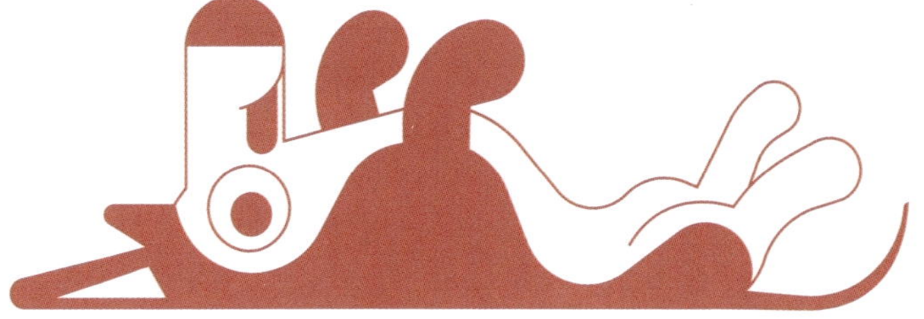

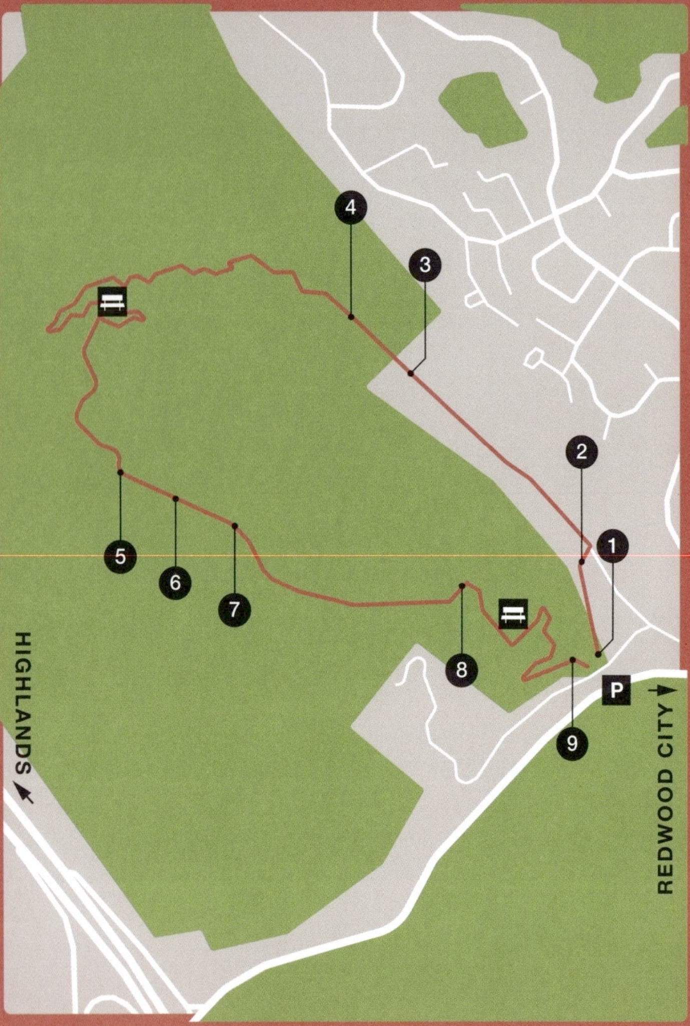

4
3
2
1
5
6
7
8
9
HIGHLANDS
REDWOOD CITY
P

P Parking

Bench

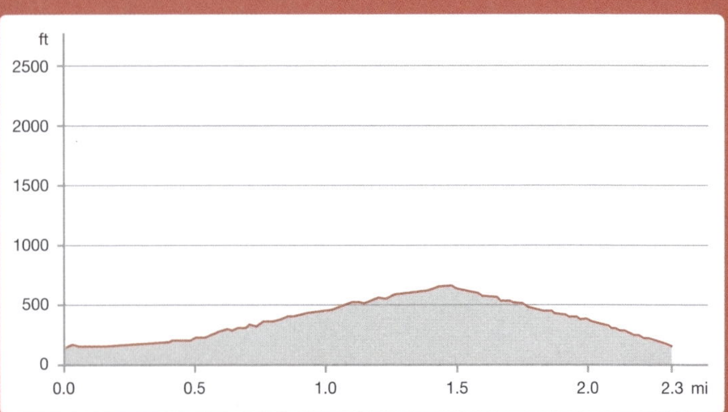

PULGAS RIDGE OPEN SPACE PRESERVE

SWEEPING RIDGELINE VIEWS WITH AN OFF-LEASH DOG AREA

REDWOOD CITY, CA

12

LENGTH
2.3 miles (loop)

TIME & MONEY
1 hour,
free

ELEVATION GAIN
400 feet

DIFFICULTY
Easy

CONDITIONS
Year-round;
partially shaded

HIGHLIGHTS
Off-leash dog area,
ridge views

ESSENTIALS

- **Find the trailhead:** From Palo Alto, follow Interstate 280 northbound towards Redwood City. In 4.6 miles, take the exit for Edgewood Road. In 0.2 miles, turn right onto Edgewood Road. In 0.8 miles, turn left on Crestview Drive and, just 0.1 miles beyond, turn left on Edmonds Road. In 0.1 miles, follow Edmonds Road left and proceed for 300 feet. You will find the entrance for Pulgas Ridge Parking Lot on your right. The trailhead is at the northeast corner of the parking lot, near the information kiosk and dog waste station.
- **Land manager:** Midpeninsula Regional Open Space (www.openspace.org)

WHY YOU'LL LOVE IT

- Large off-leash dog area
- Views of surrounding hills

Meander along an oak-covered trail to the top of Pulgas Ridge and enjoy scenic views of the Bay Area hillside as well as a 17.5-acre off-leash dog area.

Pulgas Ridge is a 366-acre preserve located near the Bay Area cities of Redwood City and San Carlos. The preserve offers over 6 miles of hiking trails among shaded canyons. At the center of the preserve sits a popular off-leash dog area. Pulgas Ridge Preserve was formerly the Hassler Health Home, a tuberculosis sanitarium owned by the City of San Francisco. Although the sanitarium was demolished in 1985, you may see remnants of buildings as you approach the Polly Geraci Trail within the first half mile of the hike.

The Polly Geraci Trail is a quiet and peaceful dirt trail that takes you up the canyon to the top of the ridge. Keep an eye out for various species of plants including toyon, which can be identified by its bright-red berries. About halfway through the Polly Geraci Trail, you'll see a wooden bench perfect for a rest and snack break. The ascent up the Polly Geraci Trail is gentle, and you'll soon see the trees open to surrounding views of the hillside. Along this ascent, you can occasionally peek through the trees and see the hills across the canyon.

After leaving the Polly Geraci Trail to the paved Hassler Trail, you'll emerge onto the ridgetop with the best views of the hillside. An open wooden fence marks the beginning of the off-leash dog area, a major feature of the Pulgas Ridge Preserve. Dogs are allowed throughout the entire fence-to-fence area of the Hassler Trail, where they can run into the taller grass and fields on either side of the trail. As you leave the Hassler Trail and turn onto the Blue Oak Trail, you'll notice signs to re-leash your dogs if you took them off-leash before.

The journey back to the parking lot is a gentle descent along a dirt trail, lined by larger rocks for the first hundred feet and shaded by trees throughout. At the parking lot, you'll find both a dog waste bin for any collectables you picked up along the way and a restroom for humans.

TURN-BY-TURN DIRECTIONS

1. From the trailhead kiosk, follow a dirt trail to the signposted junction of the Cordilleras Trail.
2. At 0.1 miles, turn left onto the signposted Cordilleras Trail.
3. At 0.4 miles, turn right through an open wooden fence toward the Polly Geraci Trail. After 50 feet, turn left and cross a bridge onto the signposted Polly Geraci Trail.
4. At 0.5 miles, continue straight on the signposted Polly Geraci Trail.
5. At 1.4 miles, turn left onto the signposted Hassler Trail.
6. At 1.5 miles, go through a gate to begin the off-leash area on the signposted Hassler Trail.
7. At 1.8 miles, stay right to continue on the Hassler Trail toward the signposted Blue Oak Trail.
8. At 1.9 miles, turn right through an open wooden fence onto the signposted Blue Oak Trail to descend back down toward the parking lot. Dogs must be on-leash on the Blue Oak Trail.
9. At 2.3 miles, arrive back at the parking lot.

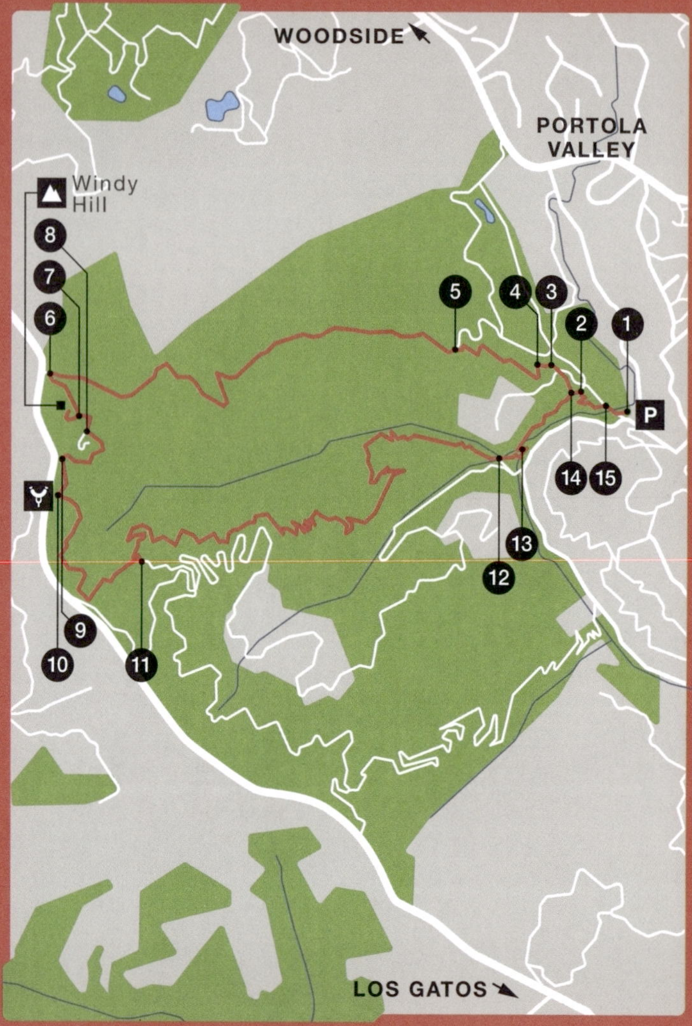

WOODSIDE
PORTOLA VALLEY
Windy Hill
1
2
3
4
5
6
7
8
9
10
11
12
13
14
15
P
LOS GATOS

P Parking   Picnic table   Mountain

ft
2500
2000
1500
1000
500
0.0
0.5
1.0
1.5
2.0
2.5
3.0
3.5
4.0
4.5
5.0
5.5
6.0
6.5
mi

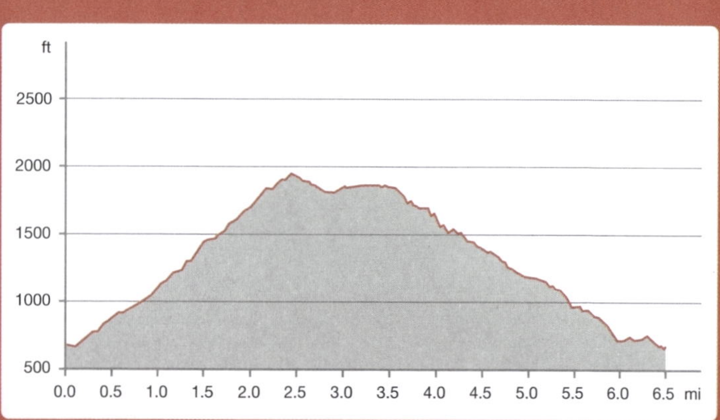

WINDY HILL

HIKE THROUGH ROLLING HILLS AND SHADED WOODLANDS

PORTOLA VALLEY, CA

13

LENGTH

6.5 miles (loop)

TIME & MONEY

3 hours,
free

ELEVATION GAIN

1,337 feet

DIFFICULTY

Moderate

CONDITIONS

Year-round;
mostly exposed

HIGHLIGHTS

Rolling grassland,
360-degree views

ESSENTIALS

- **Find the trailhead:** From San Jose, take Interstate 280 northbound. In 20 miles, take the exit for Alpine Road/Portola Valley. In 0.3 miles, turn left onto Alpine Road. In 4.0 miles, there is a small parking lot on your right on Alpine Road. If the parking lot is full, continue 200 feet down Alpine Road and make a right onto Willowbrook Drive. There is street parking available on Willowbrook Drive. Both the parking lot and street parking are convenient options; the trailhead is only 400 feet further ahead, heading west on Alpine Road from the parking lot. The trailhead will be on your right-hand side on Alpine Road.
- **Land manager:** Midpeninsula Regional Open Space (openspace.org).

WHY YOU'LL LOVE IT

- 360-degree views of rolling hills
- Gentle terrain for your dog's paws
- Loop hike with varied landscape

Hike along rolling hills to Windy Hill Summit for 360-degree views of the Santa Cruz Mountains and the surrounding Bay Area.

Windy Hill is a 1,414-acre preserve easily accessible from Bay Area cities. While many of the hikes off the famed Skyline Boulevard (Route 35) are closed off to dogs, Windy Hill welcomes our furry friends. You and your dog will enjoy hiking through diverse landscapes with gentle terrain on this loop trail.

The hike begins on the Meadow Trail, where you'll walk through gentle, grassy meadows. After a little over a half mile, you'll turn onto the Spring Ridge Trail, a wide fire road that ascends over 800 feet in one and a half miles. You'll enjoy views of the surrounding Bay Area for most of the Spring Ridge Trail. Lining the trail, you'll notice various plant species like milkmaids, pacific hound's tongue, California blackberries, and California poppies.

After a short section on the Anniversary Trail, you'll reach Windy Hill Summit. As the name suggests, the summit can be very windy, and you may see hang gliders, paragliders, or people flying kites taking advantage of the wind. Leaving Windy Hill Summit, you'll head down to shady woodlands of Douglas fir and tanoak on the Hamms Gulch Trail. About half a mile before the end of the hike, you'll cross a small stream that's a popular water stop for dogs. The amount of water in the stream depends on recent rainfall.

TURN-BY-TURN DIRECTIONS

1. From the Willowbrook trailhead kiosk, follow a dirt path right. After 200 feet, cross a wooden bridge. After another 250 feet, stay left on the dirt path following the signpost for the Meadow Trail.
2. At 0.2 miles, turn left onto the signposted Meadow Trail Driveway Bypass. After 150 feet, turn right onto the signposted Meadow Trail.
3. At 0.3 miles, continue straight at the signposted Meadow Trail.
4. At 0.4 miles, turn left to stay on the signposted Meadow Trail.
5. At 0.8 miles, turn left at the signposted Spring Ridge Trail.
6. At 2.3 miles, pass the Upper Spring Ridge trailhead kiosk and turn left onto the signposted Anniversary Trail.
7. At 2.4 miles, turn right at a bench toward the unmarked Windy Hill Summit. After 250 feet, reach Windy Hill Summit. When you're ready, turn around and retrace your steps back to the bench. At the bench, turn right onto the unmarked Anniversary Trail.
8. At 2.6 miles, pass another set of wooden benches and stay left on the Anniversary Trail.
9. At 2.9 miles, continue through a wooden gate to stay on the Anniversary Trail.
10. At 3.0 miles, reach the Anniversary Trail picnic tables and restroom. Turn left onto the signposted Lost Trail.
11. At 3.6 miles, take a sharp left onto the signposted Hamms Gulch Trail.
12. At 5.9 miles, pass through a wooden gate and turn left to continue on the Hamms Gulch Trail toward Alpine Road.
13. At 6.0 miles, cross a small stream to continue on the Hamms Gulch Trail.
14. At 6.3 miles, turn right to stay on the Hamms Gulch Trail. After 250 feet, turn right onto the Meadow Trail Driveway Bypass.
15. At 6.4 miles, turn right and cross the wooden bridge from Step 1 again. Return to the trailhead the way you came.

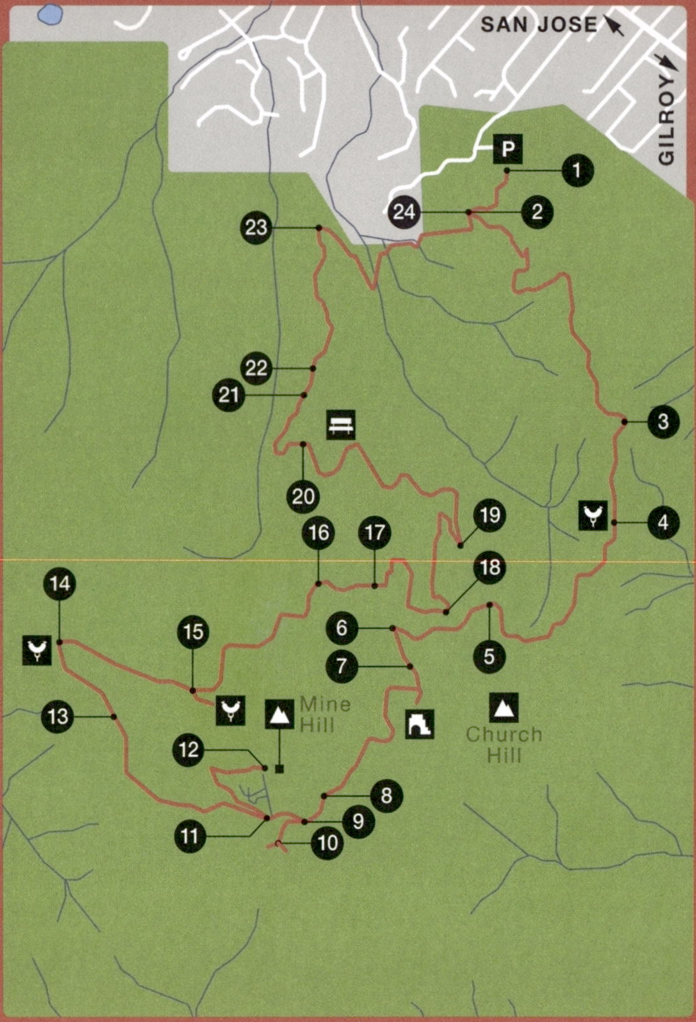

SAN JOSE
GILROY
P
1
2
3
4
5
6
7
8
9
10
11
12
13
14
15
16
17
18
19
20
21
22
23
24
Mine Hill
Church Hill

P Parking | Picnic table | Bench
Mountain | English Camp ruins

ft
2000
1500
1000
500
0
0.0
0.5
1.0
1.5
2.0
2.5
3.0
3.5
4.0
4.5
5.0
5.5
6.0
6.5
7.0
7.5 mi

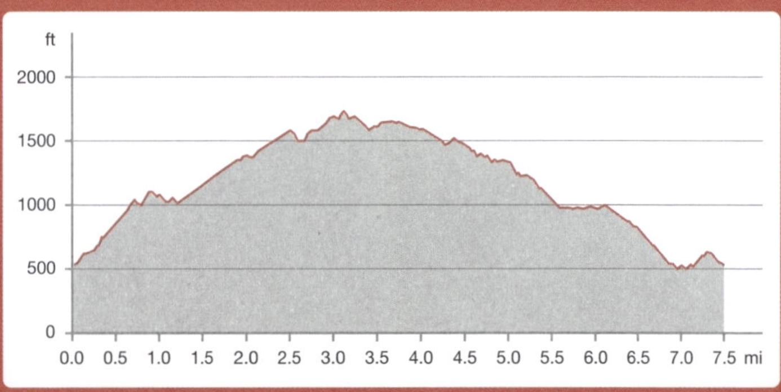

ALMADEN QUICKSILVER COUNTY PARK

EXPLORE A HISTORIC MINING COMMUNITY

SAN JOSE, CA

14

LENGTH
7.5 miles (loop)

TIME & MONEY
3 hours 45 min., free

ELEVATION GAIN
1,766 feet

DIFFICULTY
Strenuous

CONDITIONS
Year-round; partially exposed

HIGHLIGHTS
Historic mining sites, scenic overlooks

ESSENTIALS

- **Find the trailhead:** From downtown San Jose, head south on Delmas Avenue. In 0.3 miles, merge onto CA-87 south. In 4.9 miles, merge onto CA-85 north toward Mountain View. In 0.9 miles, take the exit for Almaden Expressway and then turn left onto Almaden Expressway. After 4.4 miles, turn right onto Almaden Road. In 0.6 miles, turn right onto Mockingbird Hill Lane. The parking lot will be on the left in 0.4 miles. There are trash bins and dog waste bags at the parking lot.

- **Land manager:** Santa Clara County Parks (parks.santaclaracounty.gov)

WHY YOU'LL LOVE IT

- Interpretive displays about mining ruins
- Views of hillsides and the Santa Clara Valley
- Seasonal wildflowers

Explore remnants of a quicksilver mine and learn about the area's mining history while enjoying spectacular hillside vistas.

Nestled in the foothills south of San Jose, Almaden Quicksilver County Park once housed the New Almaden mercury mine. The mine began operations in 1845 and eventually produced more than 83 million pounds of mercury. Miners used most of this mercury during the heyday of California's Gold Rush and Nevada's Comstock silver lode to help separate valuable minerals from non-valuable ones with a process called amalgamation.

Mercury production fell in the 1880s and 1890s because ore quality declined and scientists discovered a new method to separate precious metals with cyanide. New Almaden continued mining mercury on a small scale until the County Parks Department bought the land in 1973.

Your hike starts by winding through the eastern foothills of the Santa Cruz Mountains. Oak and buckeye trees line the path, providing shade for you and your dogs. In spring, you may see wildflowers such as blue dicks and monkey flowers. About three-quarters of a mile into the hike, you'll reach a small clearing where you can see the Santa Clara Valley.

When you get to the English Camp mining community, the trail is exposed over the next two miles, so it can get hot in the midday sun. About a thousand miners and their families came from Cornwall, England, and lived in English Camp. The community included a school, church, and general store. Today, only a few structures remain, but interpretive displays help illustrate buildings from the area's ruins.

Less than a mile after English Camp, you'll reach the Mine Hill Rotary Furnace. Across from the Mine Hill Rotary Furnace, you'll find a unique tree known as the Hanging Tree. The tree's name is from a story shared by Leonard Espinosa, a retired educator from a New Almaden mining family. In the late 1800s, there was an execution that took place at the tree.

After leaving the furnace and tree, you'll climb a few hundred feet up to Mine Hill, where you'll see panoramic views of the Santa Cruz Mountains. You'll hike for around a mile on the exposed trail before heading back into the shaded canopy. Around four miles into the hike, you'll reach San Cristobal Tunnel, an eerie mining tunnel built in 1866. You can't go inside it, but you can peek through the gate with a flashlight.

For the next few miles, you'll hike on a narrow connector trail back toward the parking lot. This connector trail has poison oak, but is passable, so be mindful of your steps. As you reach the end of your hike, your final historical site is the remains of the Buena Vista pumphouse. The pumphouse had a shaft that reached a depth of 2,300 feet. It pumped water out of mining tunnels so miners could reach more deposits of cinnabar or mercury ore.

TURN-BY-TURN DIRECTIONS

1. From the trailhead, head onto the signposted New Almaden Trail.
2. At 0.2 miles, turn left onto the signposted Hacienda Trail.
3. At 1.0 miles, turn right onto the signposted Capehorn Pass Trail.
4. At 1.2 miles, take the second right at the signposted junction onto the Mine Hill Trail.
5. At 1.6 miles, stay left to continue on the signposted Mine Hill Trail.
6. At 1.9 miles, turn left onto the signposted Castillero Trail.
7. At 2.0 miles, stay left at the fork. After 200 feet, reach the remains of the English Camp mining community. When you're ready, head to the flagpole in English Camp and turn left onto the signposted Castillero Trail.
8. At 2.4 miles, continue straight on the marked Castillero Trail.
9. At 2.5 miles, the trail splits into the Castillero Trail on your right and the Wood Road Trail on your left. Turn left to head onto the Wood Road Trail first; you'll come back to this junction next.
10. At 2.6 miles, reach the Mine Hill Rotary Furnace on your left and the Hanging Tree on your right. When you're done exploring, go back to the junction from Step 9 and turn left onto the marked Castillero Trail.
11. At 2.8 miles, turn right at the unmarked junction to head up to Mine Hill. The last 100 feet up to Mine Hill has loose rock, and this detour can be skipped if you or your dogs have mobility constraints.
12. At 3.1 miles, reach Mine Hill. When you're ready, return to the junction from Step 11 and turn right to continue on the Castillero Trail.
13. At 3.8 miles, continue straight on the unmarked Castillero Trail, ignoring a trail on your right.
14. At 4.0 miles, reach picnic tables on your left. Turn right onto the signposted Mine Hill Trail.
15. At 4.3 miles, turn right onto the signposted San Cristobal Mine Trail. You'll reach picnic tables and the San Cristobal Tunnel in 300 feet. When you're ready, head back to the junction and turn right to continue on the Mine Hill Trail.
16. At 4.8 miles, keep right to continue on the signposted Mine Hill Trail.
17. At 5.0 miles, continue straight onto the signposted Great Eastern Trail. Watch for poison oak along this narrow connector trail.
18. At 5.3 miles, turn left onto the signposted Day Tunnel Trail.
19. At 5.6 miles, turn left onto the signposted Randol Trail.
20. At 6.1 miles, turn right to stay on the signposted Randol Trail.
21. At 6.4 miles, pass the Buena Vista pumphouse on your right and then continue straight.
22. At 6.5 miles, continue straight onto the signposted Buena Vista Trail.
23. At 6.7 miles, turn right onto the signposted New Almaden Trail.
24. At 7.3 miles, reach the junction from Step 2 and retrace your steps back to the parking lot.

SUNOL

P

SUNOL

SAN JOSE

P Parking

Toilet

Waterfall

SUNOL WILDERNESS REGIONAL PRESERVE

OFF-LEASH HIKE TO A SCENIC GORGE

SUNOL, CA

15

LENGTH
3.9 miles (loop)

TIME & MONEY
2 hours,
parking fee

ELEVATION GAIN
395 feet

DIFFICULTY
Moderate

CONDITIONS
Year-round;
mostly exposed

HIGHLIGHTS
Waterfall,
off-leash trails

ESSENTIALS

- **Find the trailhead:** From downtown Oakland, take CA-24 east. In 0.2 miles, merge onto Interstate 980 east. In 0.5 miles, merge onto Interstate 580 east toward Hayward and continue for 24.4 miles. Take the exit for Interstate 680 south toward San Jose. In 8.2 miles, merge onto CA-84 east toward Calaveras Road/Dumbarton Bridge. In 0.4 miles, turn left to stay on CA-84 east. In 0.1 miles, continue straight onto Calaveras Road and proceed for 4.2 miles. Turn left onto Geary Road, and the parking area will be on your left in 2.0 miles. The first parking lot you'll pass is the Sunol Visitor Center lot. Continue straight for another 0.1 miles to reach a second parking lot and park here. There are trash bins and restrooms but no water source. There is a parking fee on weekends and holidays.
- **Land manager:** East Bay Regional Park District (ebparks.org)

WHY YOU'LL LOVE IT

- Seasonal waterfall in scenic gorge
- Panoramic vistas of the canyon
- Off-leash trails

Meander through oak woodland hills to a modest waterfall nestled in a scenic gorge along Alameda Creek.

The Sunol Wilderness Regional Preserve covers almost 7,000 acres between Mission Peak and the Ohlone Wilderness. Despite being only a few miles from the highway, Sunol feels like a remote park thanks to rolling hills that block out car traffic.

Your hike begins with a bridge crossing over Alameda Creek, where you'll join the Canyon View Trail. You'll climb steadily up the oak-dotted hillside, with most of the elevation gain packed into the first mile. Seasonal changes will dramatically change your hiking experience here: In spring, the hills turn green, dotted with butterfly mariposa lilies and other wildflowers; in summer, the hills start to brown, and the heat can be very intense for both you and your dogs; by late fall and into winter, the temperature will become more comfortable, but the hills stay dry and muted until the rains begin. If you hike in the summer, it's best to start early to avoid the hottest part of the day.

From roughly mid-September to the end of October, you may see tarantulas on the trail. During mating season, male tarantulas emerge from their burrows to find females. Tarantula hawk wasps, a predator, hunt tarantulas as they traverse the landscape. Tarantula hawk wasps sting and paralyze the spiders and then drag the immobilized tarantulas into burrows for their offspring.

About two miles into the hike, you'll turn onto a gravel road, which leads to Alameda Creek Overlook. Previously known as Little Yosemite, Alameda Creek Overlook is a scenic gorge with a series of small waterfalls and pools. The water levels are dependent on the season's rainfall, and while the gorge is beautiful to look at, swimming in the creek is prohibited.

Birding is exceptional in the Sunol Wilderness. Over 178 species have been identified in the park. At Alameda Creek Overlook, you may see species such as the black phoebe, Lawrence's goldfinch, and Lincoln's sparrow. Wood ducks also often swim in the creek. After you leave Alameda Creek Overlook, you'll hike for another mile to return to the parking lot. This section of the hike is relatively uneventful, following a wide gravel trail. If you're lucky though, you may see wild turkeys between here and the parking lot.

TURN-BY-TURN DIRECTIONS

1. The trail starts at an unmarked opening between the parking lot fence. After 100 feet, reach the trailhead for the Canyon View Trail.
2. At 300 feet, after crossing the bridge, turn right onto the unmarked trail. There is a trash bin and usually stocked dog-waste bags at this junction. After 50 feet, continue straight at the unmarked junction.
3. At 0.2 miles, continue straight on the Canyon View Trail. After 200 feet, turn left at the marked arrow for the Canyon View Trail. You'll start a steep ascent.
4. At 0.5 miles, walk through a livestock gate. Cattle are not always present, but if they are, leash your dog.
5. At 0.7 miles, continue straight at the signed junction for the Canyon View Trail.
6. At 1.1 miles, stay right, following the arrow sign.
7. At 1.2 miles, stay left at the unmarked junction to continue on the Canyon View Trail.
8. At 1.4 miles, continue straight at the signed junction to stay on the Canyon View Trail.
9. At 1.8 miles, turn right at the signed junction onto a gravel road.
10. At 2.3 miles, reach Alameda Creek Overlook. You can climb down carefully to explore the rocks and small waterfall, but swimming is prohibited. Use extreme caution when climbing. It may not be suitable for all dogs. When you're ready, continue on the gravel road.
11. At 2.3 miles, cross the cattle grate. There is also a trash bin here.
12. At 3.1 miles, continue straight across the cattle grate to stay on the gravel road.
13. At 3.3 miles, you've reached the opposite end of the Sunol Regional Wilderness parking lot. Continue straight alongside the paved road to return back to your car. There are signs saying, "Hikers Use Foot Path" directing you along dirt paths that run adjacent to the paved road.
14. At 3.5 miles, cross the paved road to continue on a dirt path marked with a symbol of a hiker.
15. At 3.7 miles, cross the paved road to continue on a dirt path marked by a symbol of a hiker. The parking area you started at is 300 feet ahead.

SANTA CRUZ AND MONTEREY

MORGAN HILL

P Parking

Campground

Waterfall

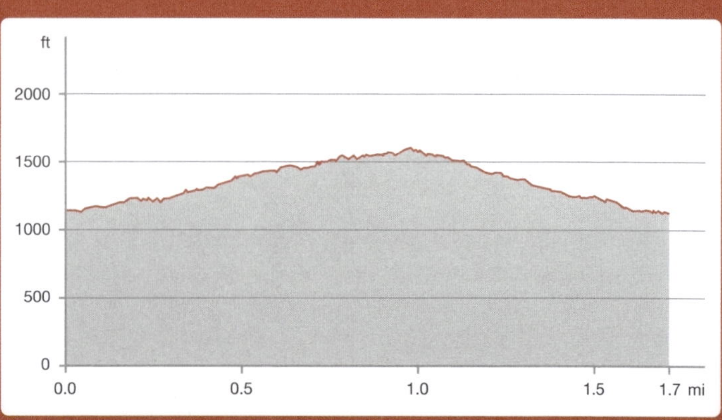

UVAS CANYON

GENTLE HIKE WITH FOUR CHARMING WATERFALLS

MORGAN HILL, CA

16

LENGTH

1.7 miles (loop)

TIME & MONEY

1 hour, pre-paid reservation fee

ELEVATION GAIN

420 feet

DIFFICULTY

Easy

CONDITIONS

Year-round; mostly shaded

HIGHLIGHTS

Waterfalls, fern-filled canyons

ESSENTIALS

- **Find the trailhead:** From San Jose, take Interstate 101 southbound. In 12 miles, take Exit 373 toward Bailey Avenue. In 0.2 miles, turn right onto Bailey Avenue. In 0.2 miles, keep left to stay on Bailey Avenue. In 3 miles, turn left onto McKean Road. In 6.2 miles, turn right onto Croy Road. In 4.3 miles, continue straight past Sveadal, a private resort belonging to the Swedish American Patriotic League, on Croy Road until you reach the park entrance 0.1 miles ahead.
- **Land manager:** Santa Clara County Parks & Recreation Department (parks.sccgov.org)

WHY YOU'LL LOVE IT

- Shaded trail
- Gentle terrain for dogs' paws
- Waterfalls to cool off in

Hike in a lush canyon on the eastern side of the Santa Cruz Mountains to four small waterfalls.

Uvas Canyon County Park is an enchanting 1,147-acre park with a rich history in present-day Morgan Hill. Uvas Canyon is located on the ancestral territory of the Amah Mutsun, Tamien Nation, and Muwekma and has a rich history. The people of the Amah villages, for example, spoke Mutsun, a language that had been used in the greater San Juan Valley for thousands of years.

Unfortunately, the arrival of Spanish missionaries in the late 1700s resulted in both the death of Indigenous peoples and loss of land. In the 1800s, Mexico won independence from Spain, and although they had promised to return the land, they instead continued to consolidate control—the nearby Rancho Las Uvas, for example, was created by a land grant in 1842. While Uvas Canyon was not part of the land grant, it shares the Uvas name. The area is named after the once abundant wild grapes in the area (uva means "grape" in Spanish). Today, there are multiple efforts like the Amah Mutsun Land Trust to restore Indigenous stewardship of ancestral lands.

The trailhead starts past the well-maintained restrooms and water fountain. As you head on the Waterfall Loop Trail, you'll go up a short

set of stone stairs to Uvas Canyon Bridge, which overlooks the six-foot-tall Granuja Falls. You may see California blackberries and Himalayan blackberries along the trail here, which typically fruit in late summer. While California blackberries are a native plant, Himalayan blackberries are an invasive species that are native to Armenia and northern Iran. California blackberries have slender vines with three leaflets, while Himalayan blackberries have five leaflets with large thorns.

After climbing a gentle ascent for about half a mile, you'll see three waterfalls in short succession: Black Rock Falls, Upper Falls, and Basin Falls. The waterfalls are very dependent on rainfall, so they'll be most picturesque after heavy rain. Between Black Rock Falls and Upper Falls, you'll find the Myrtle Flats Rest Site, which has a picnic table and is a good opportunity to listen to the sounds of the park. The area supports plenty of plant species and wildlife, including black-tailed deer, Steller's jay (which is closely related to the blue jay), and garter snakes.

On your way back to the parking lot, you'll pass several camping and picnic sites. Camping at Uvas Canyon is a great family- and dog-friendly option with flush toilets and running water. There are 2 dogs allowed per campsite, and dogs are allowed everywhere in the park, as long as they're on a 6-foot or shorter leash.

TURN-BY-TURN DIRECTIONS

1. The hike begins near the bathrooms at a sign marked for the Waterfall Loop Nature Trail. After 200 feet, turn right, following the signpost for the Waterfall Loop Nature Trail.
2. At 0.1 miles, turn left at the sign marked "Waterfall Loop Nature Trail, Start Here." After 150 feet, turn left onto the signposted Swanson Creek Trail and then cross the Uvas Canyon Bridge. The first waterfall, Granuja Falls, will be visible from the bridge on your right.
3. At 0.2 miles, continue straight on the signposted Waterfall Loop Trail.
4. At 0.5 miles, Black Rock Falls will be on your right.
5. At 0.6 miles, continue straight on the signposted Waterfall Loop Trail.
6. At 0.7 miles, reach a signposted area with a picnic table, called Myrtle Flats. The trail will split here to both Upper Falls and Basin Falls. Go to Upper Falls first by turning left to cross an unmarked bridge. When you're ready, go back across the bridge and turn right onto the signposted Basin Falls Trail.
7. At 0.9 miles, reach Basin Falls. After enjoying the view, return the way you came, back to the parking lot.
8. At 1.3 miles, reach the trail split from Step 3. Take the trail on the right (different from the trail you hiked out on) to head back to the parking lot, following a sign for the parking lot.

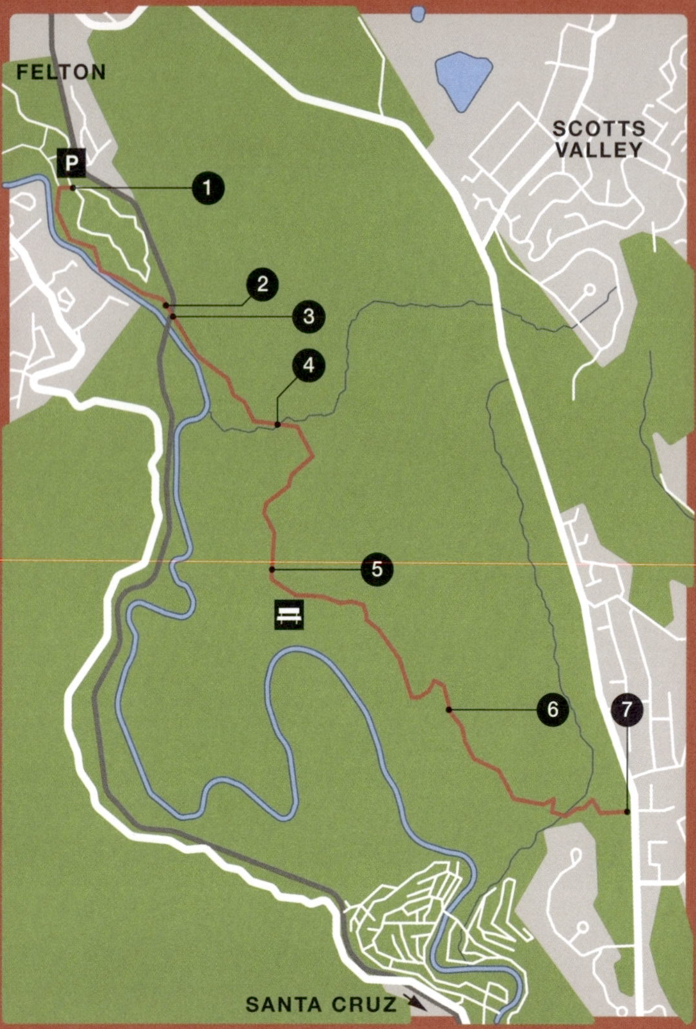

FELTON
SCOTTS VALLEY
SANTA CRUZ
P
1
2
3
4
5
6
7

P Parking

Bench

ft
2000
1500
1000
500
0
0.0
1.0
2.0
3.0
4.0
5.0
6.0
6.4 mi

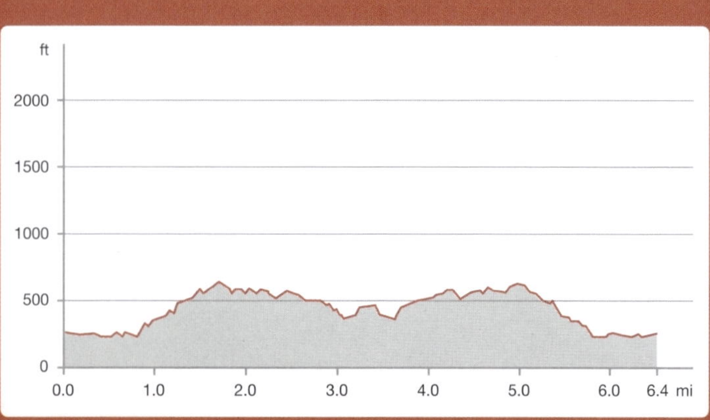

HENRY COWELL REDWOODS STATE PARK

REDWOOD TREES IN THE SANTA CRUZ MOUNTAINS

FELTON, CA

17

LENGTH
6.4 miles (loop)

TIME & MONEY
2 hours 15 min., parking fee

ELEVATION GAIN
679 feet

DIFFICULTY
Moderate

CONDITIONS
Year-round; shade

HIGHLIGHTS
Redwood trees, historical park

ESSENTIALS

- **Find the trailhead:** From San Jose, take CA-17 South toward Santa Cruz. In 23 miles, take the exit for Mount Hermon Road. In 0.2 miles, turn right onto Mount Hermon Road. In 3.5 miles, turn right onto Graham Hill Road. In 0.2 miles, turn left onto Highway 9. In 0.6 miles, turn left onto North Big Trees Park Road. The parking lot is at the end of North Big Trees Park Road, 0.7 miles ahead.
- **Land manager:** California State Parks (parks.ca.gov)

WHY YOU'LL LOVE IT

- Historically significant old-growth coastal redwoods
- Easy, paved path makes the trail accessible for dogs with less mobility
- Out-and-back trail is flexible for hikers who need a shorter distance

Stroll on the Pipeline Road Trail through historic coastal redwood trees in the popular Henry Cowell Redwoods State Park.

Henry Cowell Redwoods State Park is one of the most renowned parks in Santa Cruz County for its 40-acre old-growth redwood grove and its proximity to urban areas like Santa Cruz. As you walk from the parking lot to head onto the Pipeline Road Trail, you'll see a large cross-section display of the rings of a 2,200-year-old redwood tree. The display is labeled the "Tale of the Rings." While examining the different rings, you'll find dates with historic events spanning centuries. This exhibit reminds us of the deep history inside the park and the age of the redwoods around us.

The entire Pipeline Road Trail is paved and bisects the north and south ends of the park. Within the first half mile, you'll reach the San Lorenzo River. Because of the sensitive species in the river, dogs are not allowed in. Henry Cowell Redwoods State Park is on ancestral lands of the Awaswas-speaking Ohlone peoples, the Sayante tribe. They fished for steelhead and salmon in the San Lorenzo River and would exchange the fish for other resources, such as acorns and obsidian, with neighboring tribes. Colonial violence displaced all the Sayante peoples, and there are no known survivors. However, neighboring tribes continue their stewardship in tribute to the Sayante, ensuring their history and contributions are always remembered.

After you pass the San Lorenzo River, the Pipeline Road Trail heads deeper into the redwood forest. There was once an estimated 2 million acres of old-growth coastal redwood trees along the California coast. Today, only an estimated 5 percent of the original 2 million acres remain. The Pipeline Road Trail has a mix of both old-growth and second-growth redwoods. Second-growth redwoods were naturally regenerated after extensive logging in the 19th and early 20th centuries, as opposed to old-growth, which have never been logged.

About a mile and a half into the hike, you'll reach an overlook bench at a clearing in the trees that provides a great opportunity to look down at the vast redwood trees making up the south end of the park. You may also notice other tree and plant species surrounding the redwoods, such as white alder, tanoak, and fern. Despite its name, tanoak is not a true oak but belongs to the beech family. It produces acorns that are an essential food source for wildlife such as squirrels and deer in the redwoods.

The second half of the hike continues to gently wind through Henry Cowell. The crowds tend to thin out here, and you'll have much of the forest to yourself. You may notice fallen redwoods that provide the perfect habitat for insects such as beetles. You may also see moss growing on the bark of a redwood tree, which helps retain moisture. Redwood tree bark is filled with tannic acids that provide the tree protection against insects and fungi, and help with the tree's longevity.

TURN-BY-TURN DIRECTIONS

1. From the visitor center, follow the sign to the Pipeline Road Trail. At 300 feet, stay left at the sign to stay on the Pipeline Road Trail.
2. At 0.5 miles, continue straight at the intersection to stay on the Pipeline Road Trail.
3. At 0.6 miles, reach the San Lorenzo River on the right of the trail. There are numerous entry points into the San Lorenzo River for humans, but dogs must stay on the Pipeline Road Trail (pavement).
4. At 1.0 miles, continue straight at the marked intersection to stay on the Pipeline Road Trail.
5. At 1.5 miles, continue straight to stay on the signposted Pipeline Road Trail.
6. At 2.3 miles, continue straight to stay on the signposted Pipeline Road Trail.
7. At 3.1 miles, reach the end of the Pipeline Road Trail. Return the same way you came back to the parking lot, where there are restrooms and water fountains.

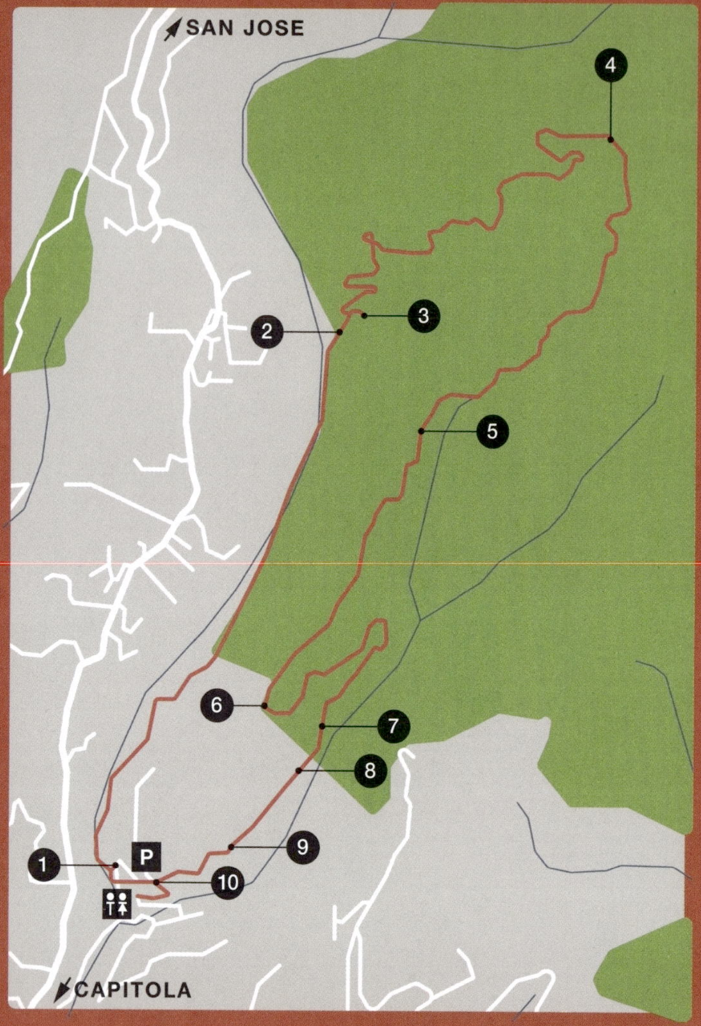

SAN JOSE

4

3

2

5

6

7

8

9

1

10

P

CAPITOLA

P Parking

Toilet

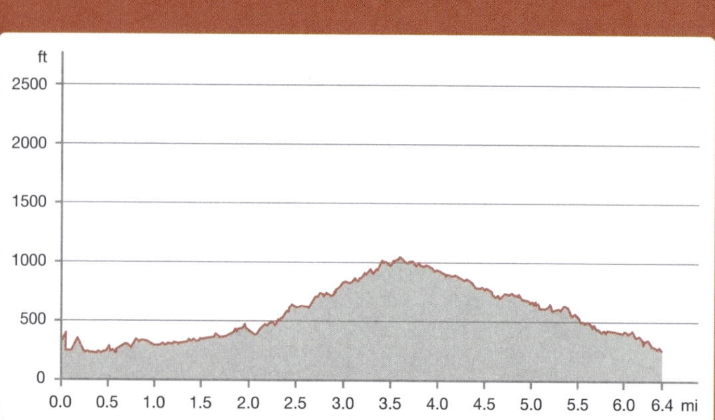

LAND OF MEDICINE BUDDHA

BUDDHIST RETREAT CENTER IN THE REDWOODS

SOQUEL, CA

18

LENGTH
6.4 miles (loop)

TIME & MONEY
2 hours 45 min, free

ELEVATION GAIN
849 feet

DIFFICULTY
Moderate

CONDITIONS
Year-round from 9 a.m.–5 p.m.; mostly shaded

HIGHLIGHTS
Buddhist artifacts, redwood trees

ESSENTIALS

- **Find the trailhead:** From downtown San Jose, take Interstate 280 north. In 2.3 miles, exit and merge onto CA-17 south toward Santa Cruz. After 0.8 miles, merge onto CA-17 south. Continue for 25.9 miles, then exit onto CA-1 south toward Watsonville/Monterey. In 3.9 miles, exit for Bay Avenue toward Porter Street. In 400 feet, turn left onto Bay Avenue, which turns into Porter Street in 100 feet. After 350 feet, turn right onto South Main Street. In 1.1 miles, keep right onto Glen Haven Road. In 0.4 miles, keep right again onto Prescott Road. In 1.0 miles, Prescott Road curves right into the parking lot on Greenwood Lane. The Land of Medicine Buddha can get crowded on holidays and weekends, and its small parking lot prioritizes visitors attending programs. Plan to arrive early if you're visiting during these times. There are restrooms and trash bins by the gift shop.

- **Land manager:** Land of Medicine Buddha (landofmedicinebuddha.org)

WHY YOU'LL LOVE IT

- Sacred sites for spiritual connection
- Mostly shaded to protect from overheating
- Peaceful and quiet scenery

Deepen your spiritual connection as you hike through the trails of the Land of Medicine Buddha, surrounded by towering redwoods and sacred symbols.

Founded in 1991 by Lama Thubten Yeshe and Lama Zopa Rinpoche, the Land of Medicine Buddha is a 108-acre sanctuary nestled amidst the Santa Cruz redwoods. The sanctuary welcomes visitors to engage in Buddhist spiritual programs such as retreats or meditation classes. In addition to these programs, there are miles of hiking trails within the property that pass by sacred sites, including shrines, prayer wheels, and prayer flags.

Your hike begins at the trailhead, marked by a set of prayer flags. These flags come in five colors representing the five elements, typically strung in the following order: blue for sky and space, white for air and wind, red for fire, green for water, and yellow for earth. Many Buddhists believe that as the winds blow through the flags, it carries the prayers and energy into an "all-pervading space"—a reminder that space is everywhere, not just the sky above us.

As you head into the redwoods for the first half of the hike, you'll pass more prayer flags hung across the redwood trees. As the trail climbs to about a thousand feet, the towering redwoods give way to more open oak- and shrub-covered hillsides. You may hear birds such as Steller's jays and band-tailed pigeons. Band-tailed pigeons are California's only native pigeons and have lighter blue-gray heads. Rock pigeons—the species you typically see in urban areas—are non-native and were brought to North America in 1606.

About five miles in, you'll reach a small, heartwarming memorial area honoring those who have passed. Framed photos and mementos pay tribute to loved ones—especially beloved dogs—making it a peaceful and reflective spot. You're welcome to add your own memorial if you feel called to do so. A few hundred feet farther, you'll see a sign that shares the tale of the Bodhisattva and the Hungry Tigress, a story of compassion and selflessness. As you near the end of the loop trail, you'll find more signs with Buddhist verses, such as Verse Five of the Eight Verses of Thought Transformation, which teaches humility and kindness in the face of mistreatment.

After, you'll arrive at the eastern side of the paved grounds. As you head west toward the parking lot, you'll pass a prayer wheel, Ksitigarbha statue, and a large Namgyalma Bell. Prayer wheels typically contain mantras; spin it clockwise to spread blessings to the world. In Buddhism, Ksitigarbha, known as the "Essence of Earth," makes vows to help those facing serious health and financial hardships. The Namgyalma Bell symbolizes purification and a long life; Buddhists believe its sound removes negative karma. Finally, as you reach the parking lot, you'll see a second prayer wheel called the Great Prayer Wheel.

TURN-BY-TURN DIRECTIONS

1. From the parking lot entrance, cross the street to an unmarked dirt path. You'll see prayer flags overhead at the trailhead. Continue straight onto the 6 Mile Trail Loop.
2. At 1.3 miles, keep right at the "Hiking Trail" sign to stay on the trail.
3. At 1.4 miles, keep right again at another "Hiking Trail" sign to stay on the trail.
4. At 3.2 miles, pass under a set of prayer flags. At this unmarked junction, keep right to continue on the trail.
5. At 4.1 miles, keep left at the arrows to continue on the trail. Both the left and right trail take you to the same location, but our route goes left.
6. At 4.8 miles, turn left at the signed junction for the 2 Mile Trail.
7. At 5.3 miles, reach a memorial area honoring those who have passed. When you're ready, continue straight, back on the trail.
8. At 5.8 miles, reach a sign signaling the start of Land of Medicine Buddha private property. Keep left onto the 8 Verses Loop Trail, heading back toward the parking lot.
9. At 6.0 miles, turn right at the junction for the marked "Exit" sign.
10. At 6.2 miles, reach a pet waste station and a prayer wheel, Ksitigarbha statue, and a large Namgyalma Bell. After taking your time at these stops, continue straight toward the "Exit" sign, down a paved road back to the parking lot. There is a second prayer wheel by the parking lot.

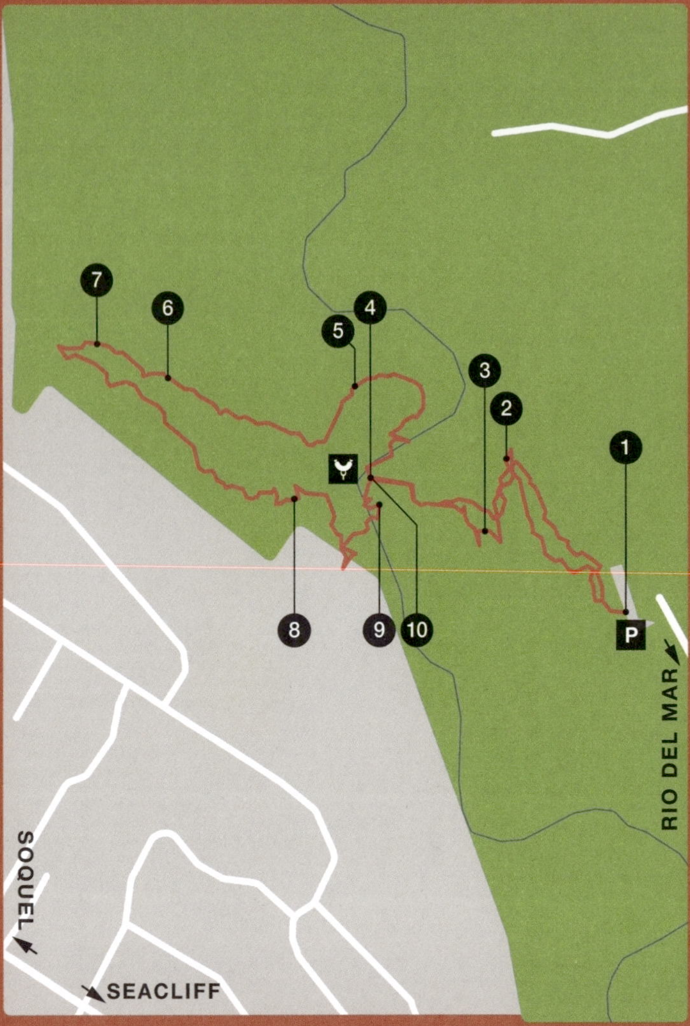

7
6
5
4
3
2
1
8
9
10
P
RIO DEL MAR
SOQUEL
SEACLIFF

P Parking

Picnic area

ft
2000
1500
1000
500
0
0.0
0.5
1.0
1.5
2.0
2.4 mi

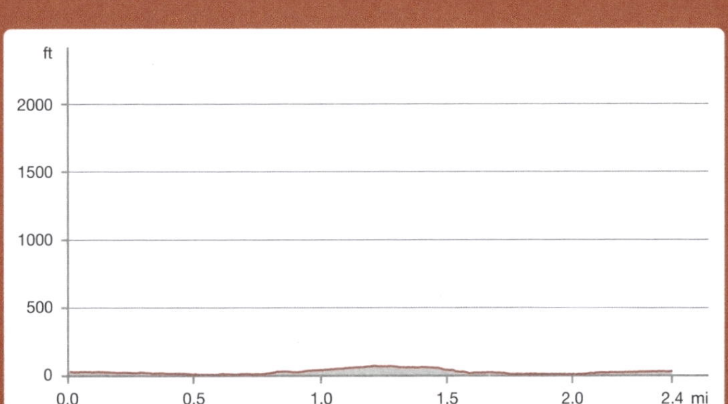

FOREST OF NISENE MARKS

WALK AMONG OLD-GROWTH REDWOOD TREES

APTOS, CA

19

LENGTH
1.4 miles
(lollipop loop)

TIME & MONEY
40 min.,
parking fee

ELEVATION GAIN
270 feet

DIFFICULTY
Moderate

CONDITIONS
Year-round;
shaded

HIGHLIGHTS
Redwood
trees

ESSENTIALS

- **Find the trailhead:** From San Jose, take CA-17 South toward Santa Cruz. In 25.9 miles, take the exit for CA-1 South toward Watsonville/ Monterey. In 6.4 miles, take Exit 435 for State Park Drive. In 0.3 miles, turn left onto State Park Drive. In 0.3 miles, turn right onto Soquel Drive. In 0.5 miles, turn left onto Aptos Creek Road and continue for 0.8 miles. Immediately after you pass the entrance kiosk, the parking lot will be on your left.
- **Land manager:** California State Parks (parks.ca.gov)

WHY YOU'LL LOVE IT

- Creek for your dogs to cool off
- Quiet and less-traveled trails

Stroll through beautiful redwood trees along the quiet Old Growth Loop at the Forest of Nisene Marks.

Nestled in the Santa Cruz Mountains near Aptos, the Forest of Nisene Marks is an example of redwood forest recovery from extensive logging between 1883 to 1923. The Old Growth Loop takes you through dense redwood forests, with a brief section of old-growth redwood trees and stops at Aptos Creek.

From the parking lot, you'll walk along a shady trail among tall redwood trees. Eighty percent of the park is covered in the coastal redwood species that are between 80 to 120 years old. Earthquake faults running through the park gradually alter the park's geology and the structure of the trees over time—the shifting ground can cause trees to tilt, develop stress cracks, or adapt their root systems to maintain stability.

Within the first half mile, you'll reach Aptos Creek, a prominent water source that flows through deep canyons, carving out valleys and nourishing the redwoods, ferns, and diverse plant life that thrive along its banks. Your dogs will have an opportunity to cool off in the flowing water before continuing across a wooden bridge. The water level of the creek is highly dependent on rainfall, and during heavy storms, it may not be possible to cross due to flooding.

The trail then goes deeper into the redwoods. Just after an area called the Twisted Grove, you'll find a modest section of old-growth redwood trees, but we'll be staying left to continue on the Old Growth Loop. As you get deeper into this section of the Old Growth Loop, the trail becomes less traveled, and you may see more species of wildlife, including the popular banana slug.

Around one mile in, you'll reach what remains of the Advocate Tree. The Advocate Tree, which fell down in 2017 after a period of storms, was a majestic, one-thousand-year-old tree standing at 253 feet with a circumference of 39 feet. Unfortunately, a "goosepen," or hollow opening, had formed in the tree's heartwood due to fires. This goosepen may have contributed to the tree's instability at the time of the storms.

After passing the Advocate Tree, you'll reach the southern end of the Aptos Creek section. A fallen-over tree bridge will help you cross the creek without getting wet. While you're here, you may hear sounds of the American dipper, a small, grayish songbird that is typically found near freshwater. You may see them dipping and bobbing for food near moving streams, which gives them the "dipper" name. This final creek crossing will take you to the end of the Old Growth Loop.

TURN-BY-TURN DIRECTIONS

1. From the parking lot, pass the restrooms and continue straight on the unmarked trail. After 50 feet, reach the Split Stuff Trail sign and turn right, following the arrow for the Old Growth Loop. After another 150 feet, follow the trail left to stay on the signposted Split Stuff Trail.
2. At 0.1 miles, turn left onto the signposted Aptos Rancho Trail, following the arrow for the Old Growth Loop.
3. At 0.2 miles, turn right at the sign pointing toward the Old Growth Loop. This is a connector trail that takes you to the start of the Old Growth Loop.
4. At 0.3 miles, reach Aptos Creek. Cross the wooden bridge and reach a sign for the Old Growth Loop—this is the start of the Old Growth Loop. The sign has directions to complete the loop both right and left—turn right toward the Twisted Grove.
5. At 0.4 miles, keep left to stay on the Old Growth Loop.
6. At 0.6 miles, at an unmarked fork, keep left.
7. At 0.7 miles, keep left at a second unmarked fork.
8. At 0.9 miles, turn right at the signposted junction for the Advocate Tree.
9. At 1.0 miles, reach the Advocate Tree, which has fallen over from a storm. Descend to Aptos Creek and use a fallen tree to cross.
10. At 1.1 miles, reach the junction from Step 4, closing the Old Growth Loop. Turn right to cross the wooden bridge from Step 4 and head back to the parking lot, retracing your steps.

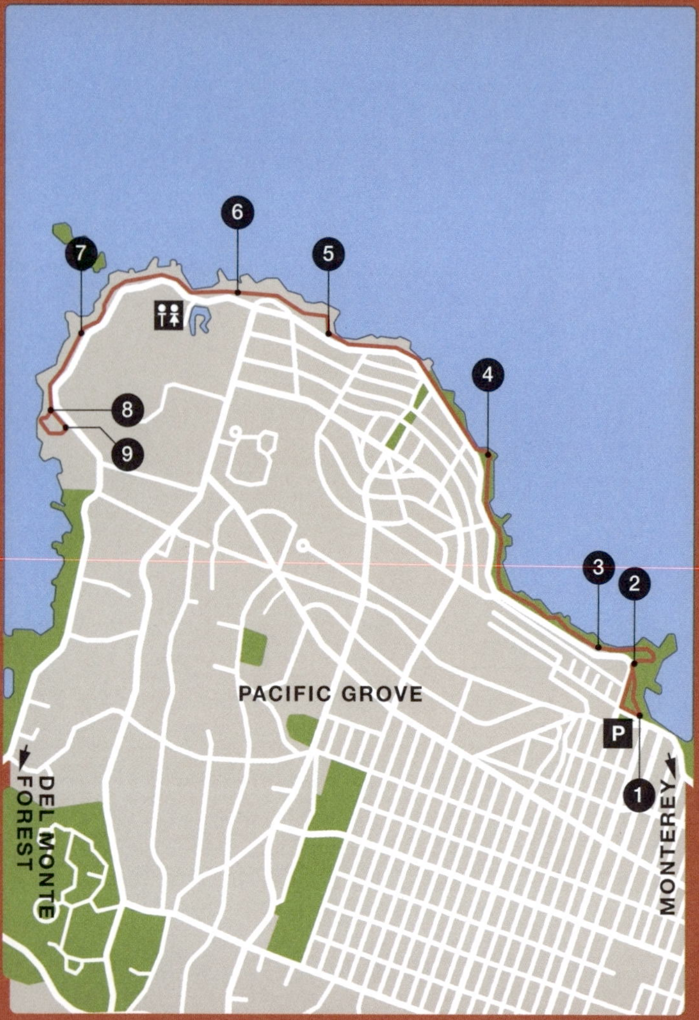

6
7
5
4
8
9
3
2
PACIFIC GROVE
P
1
DEL MONTE FOREST
MONTEREY

P Parking

Toilet

ft
2500
2000
1500
1000
500
0
0.0
0.5
1.0
1.5
2.0
2.5
3.0
3.5
4.0
4.3 mi

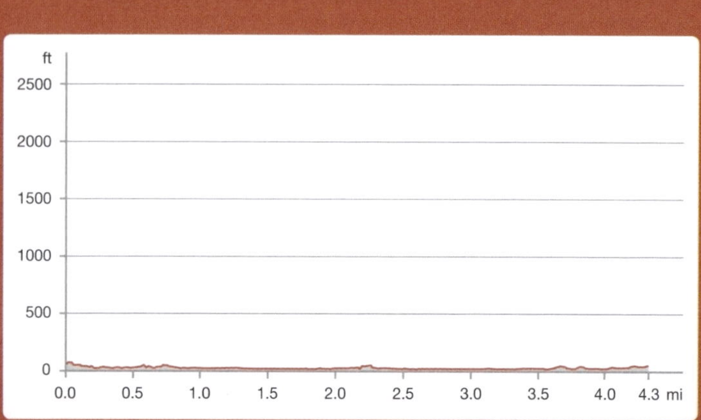

PACIFIC GROVE

EXPLORE THE FAMOUS MONTEREY COASTLINE

PACIFIC GROVE, CA

20

LENGTH
4.3 miles (round trip)

TIME & MONEY
1 hour 45 min, free

ELEVATION GAIN
8 feet

DIFFICULTY
Easy

CONDITIONS
Year-round; exposed, coastal weather

HIGHLIGHTS
Ocean views, coastal and marine wildlife

ESSENTIALS

- **Find the trailhead:** From downtown San Jose, take CA-87 south. In 4 miles, merge onto CA-85 south toward Gilroy. In 5.6 miles, merge onto US-101 south. In 39.7 miles, exit for CA-156 west toward Monterey/Peninsula, then merge onto CA-156 west. In 6.1 miles, continue onto CA-1 south. In 11.7 miles, exit onto Del Monte Avenue toward Pacific Grove, then merge onto Del Monte Avenue. In 1.6 miles, keep right onto Lighthouse Avenue. In 1.4 miles, Lighthouse Avenue becomes Central Avenue—continue straight onto Central Avenue. In 0.7 miles, turn right onto 13th Street. After 450 feet, turn left onto Ocean View Boulevard. Parking will be 0.3 miles ahead on your right. There are restrooms, trash bins, and water fountains at the cafe adjacent to the parking lot.

- **Land manager:** City of Pacific Grove (cityofpacificgrove.gov) and California State Parks (parks.ca.gov)

WHY YOU'LL LOVE IT

- Well-maintained trail for dogs' paws
- Interpretive displays
- Comfortable temperature for dogs on most days

Search for marine wildlife in the waves and tide pools as you walk along the coast from Lovers Point to the Great Tide Pool.

Your hike will follow a well-maintained but mixed-terrain path that runs along the coastline of the Monterey Bay National Marine Sanctuary, a thriving habitat teeming with diverse plants and marine wildlife. Monterey Bay is one of the world's most biologically productive ecosystems due to a phenomenon known as upwelling, where a unique underwater geography brings nutrient-rich waters from the deep ocean to the surface. Bring binoculars on your hike to spot a variety of species off the Pacific Grove coastline including seabirds, sea otters, and migrating whales.

You'll begin at Lovers Point, a picturesque 4.4-acre park in Pacific Grove featuring a beach cove and rocky cliffs. While dogs are not allowed on the beach at Lovers Point, there are often people enjoying the sand or swimming. Along the trail, look out for seabirds such as Brandt's and pelagic cormorants. Brandt's cormorants are slightly larger and often dive for food in groups in deeper waters, whereas pelagic cormorants are more solitary, typically hunting alone or in pairs.

After a quarter mile, you'll reach Perkins Park. This section of the coastline was originally overgrown and infested with poison oak, but Hayes Perkins, a self-appointed "adventurer" who retired in Pacific Grove, transformed the area by planting fluorescent-purple ice plants in the 1950s. The stunning color of the ice plants, which typically bloom in late spring, has attracted many visitors over the years–*National Geographic* has even published photographs of the park. However, ice plants are also an invasive species and can crowd out many rare plants.

As you meander past Perkins Park to Otter Point over the next half mile, you may see sea otters floating in the ocean, using tools like rocks to crush open shellfish for food. The nearby Monterey Bay Aquarium features sea otters as a key attraction, showcasing their role in the marine ecosystem to help conservation efforts. Sea otters are on the endangered list after being hunted nearly to extinction in the 1920s for their fur. In fact, all living sea otters today are descendents from around fifty sea otters that survived the mass hunting frenzy in Big Sur in 1938.

After Otter Point, you'll merge onto the Point Pinos Coastal Trail, the outcome of a construction project to make this section of the trail safer and more accessible. This section of the hike is a good place to spot whales and dolphins. Gray whales are more common in the winter and spring, while you can see Risso's dolphins year-round.

Your final stops are two tide pools, which you'll want to explore during low tide. You may spot hermit crabs, abalone, mussels, and starfish nestled in the tide pool rocks. Low tide times change daily with the moon, so check a local tide chart online before you go.

TURN-BY-TURN DIRECTIONS

1. The trail starts at the south end of Lovers Point. Follow the sidewalk right, onto Ocean View Boulevard.
2. At 0.1 miles, the sidewalk transitions to a dirt trail along Lovers Point. Explore Lovers Point on your right; when you're ready, continue left on the sandy path running parallel to Ocean View Boulevard.
3. At 0.3 miles, reach the start of Perkins Park; continue straight on the unmarked path.
4. At 0.8 miles, reach Otter Point; continue straight on the unmarked path.
5. At 1.3 miles, the trail joins the Point Pinos Coastal Trail, a segment of the California Coastal Trail.
6. At 1.5 miles, reach a sign for the Whale Trail on your right. The trail continues straight onto a boardwalk before returning to a sandy path.
7. At 1.9 miles, there's an opening down to the tide pools on your right. Check out the tide pools, then when you're ready, continue straight.
8. At 2.1 miles, turn right to follow the sandy path to the Great Tide Pool.
9. At 2.2 miles, reach the Great Tide Pool. When you're ready, return the way you came back to Lovers Point.

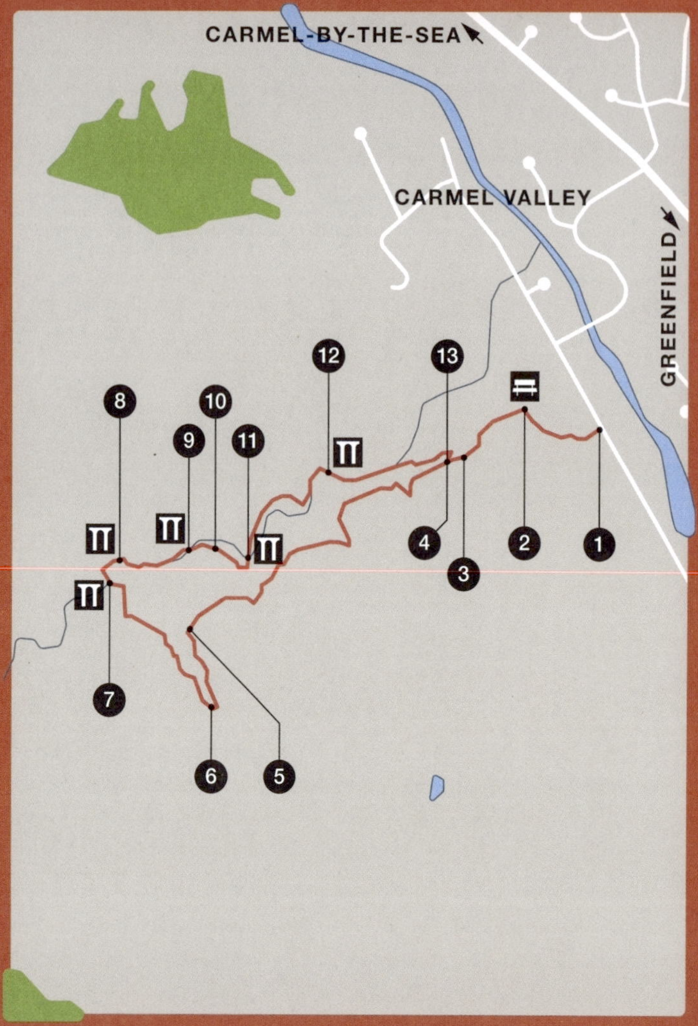

CARMEL-BY-THE-SEA
CARMEL VALLEY
GREENFIELD
1
2
3
4
5
6
7
8
9
10
11
12
13

Bench
Bridge

ft
2000
1500
1000
500
0
0.0
0.5
1.0
1.5
2.0
2.5
3.0
3.5 mi

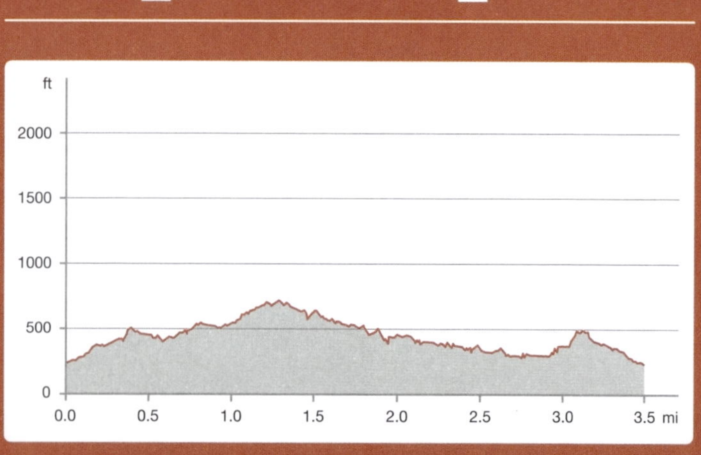

GARLAND REGIONAL PARK

CREEKSIDE JAUNT THROUGH A REDWOOD FOREST

CARMEL VALLEY, CA

21

LENGTH

3.2 miles (lollipop loop)

TIME & MONEY

1 hour 40 min., free

ELEVATION GAIN

609 feet

DIFFICULTY

Moderate

CONDITIONS

Footbridges April – November, mostly shaded

HIGHLIGHTS

Creek crossings, redwood trees

ESSENTIALS

- **Find the trailhead:** From San Jose, take Interstate 101 southbound. In 58.2 miles, take Exit 327 to merge onto CA-68 West. In 10.4 miles, turn left onto Laureles Grade. In 5.8 miles, turn left onto West Carmel Valley Road. In 0.7 miles, turn right onto Boronda Road. In 0.6 miles, turn left onto East Garzas Road and proceed for 0.2 miles. A sign for the trailhead will be on the right, and street parking is available along East Garzas Road.
- **Land manager:** Monterey Peninsula Regional Park District (mprpd.org)

WHY YOU'LL LOVE IT

- Multiple creek crossings to splash around in
- Mostly shaded to protect from overheating
- Gentle terrain for dogs' paws

Explore a redwood forest in Carmel Valley where dogs can splash in a creek that runs through the forest.

Garland Regional Park is the gem of Carmel Valley, situated 15 minutes from the historic Carmel-by-the-Sea. Purchased in 1975 from William Garland II, Garland Regional Park was the first piece of land to become a part of the Monterey Peninsula Regional Park District. William Garland II reduced the purchase price below fair market value as a way to gift a portion of the park.

For this hike, you'll explore the Garzas Canyon area, where Las Garzas Creek runs through beautiful redwood forests. The hike starts right off East Garzas Road, where there are trash cans and typically dog poop bags available for use. Around a quarter mile into the hike, you'll reach a bench with views overlooking Carmel Valley. While the nearby Monterey area has more rainy and foggy days, Carmel Valley has over 300 days of sunshine per year thanks to its inland location and the Santa Lucia mountains blocking most of that misty marine layer. The sunny days and cooler nights, added with the mineral-rich soil from being close to the ocean, make Carmel Valley a fantastic wine-growing region, especially for Cabernet Sauvignon and Merlot varietals.

You'll head into the canyon along the partially shaded Garzas Canyon Trail and Terrace Trail. Keep an eye on the sky when the path opens up on the Terrace Trail—you may catch a glimpse of a red-tailed hawk flying above you.

Once you reach the Redwood Canyon Trail, your surroundings will change from ridge views to a dense redwood forest. Although dogs are allowed off-leash, make sure they are under voice control and do not trample the plant species here, including giant trillium, toothwort, and woodland star. These flowering plants thrive in moist, shaded soils of redwood forests and are an important part of the forest's ecosystem. However, they are delicate and can be easily disturbed or damaged. Giant trilliums, for example, are slow-growing and can take five to seven years to bloom.

For the last half of the hike, you'll enjoy the highlight of this outing—crossing Las Garzas Creek a total of six times. Las Garzas Creek bisects Garland Regional Park and provides a fantastic opportunity for your dogs to splash around and cool off. The first two footbridges are permanent and can be crossed year-round. However, the third to sixth footbridges are seasonal and are generally installed from April to November. The Monterey Peninsula Regional Park District typically posts status updates about the footbridges on their website and social media and includes physical signage on the trailhead kiosk. When the footbridges are not installed, you can either cross the creek by directly stepping into the water, if it's safe to do so, or you'll need to turn around and return the way you came.

TURN-BY-TURN DIRECTIONS

1. From the trailhead kiosk on East Garzas Road, head straight for 150 feet. At 150 feet, continue straight on the signposted Garzas Canyon Trail.
2. At 0.2 miles, reach a bench where you can admire the views of Carmel Valley.
3. At 0.3 miles, stay right to continue on the signposted Garzas Canyon Trail.
4. At 0.4 miles, turn left onto the signposted Terrace Trail.
5. At 1.2 miles, turn left onto the unmarked Redwood Canyon Trail. After 200 feet, continue straight on the unmarked Redwood Canyon Trail, ignoring a trail on the left.
6. At 1.4 miles, turn right at the signposted junction to stay on the Redwood Canyon Trail.
7. At 1.8 miles, cross the Las Garzas Creek on the foot bridge. This is a great spot for dogs to cool off in the water.
8. At 1.9 miles, cross the Las Garzas Creek on another footbridge. After 100 feet, cross the third footbridge across Las Garzas Creek. This is the first seasonal footbridge that gets taken down sometime in November.
9. At 2.0 miles, cross the fourth footbridge across Las Garzas Creek.
10. At 2.1 miles, stay left on the unmarked Redwood Canyon Trail.
11. At 2.2 miles, cross the fifth footbridge across the Las Garzas Creek. After 150 feet, turn right onto the signposted Garzas Canyon Trail.
12. At 2.5 miles, cross the last footbridge across the Las Garzas Creek.
13. At 2.9 miles, turn left at the signpost from Step 4 toward East Garzas Road and head back to the trailhead kiosk, retracing your steps.

YOSEMITE AND SIERRA NEVADA FOOTHILLS

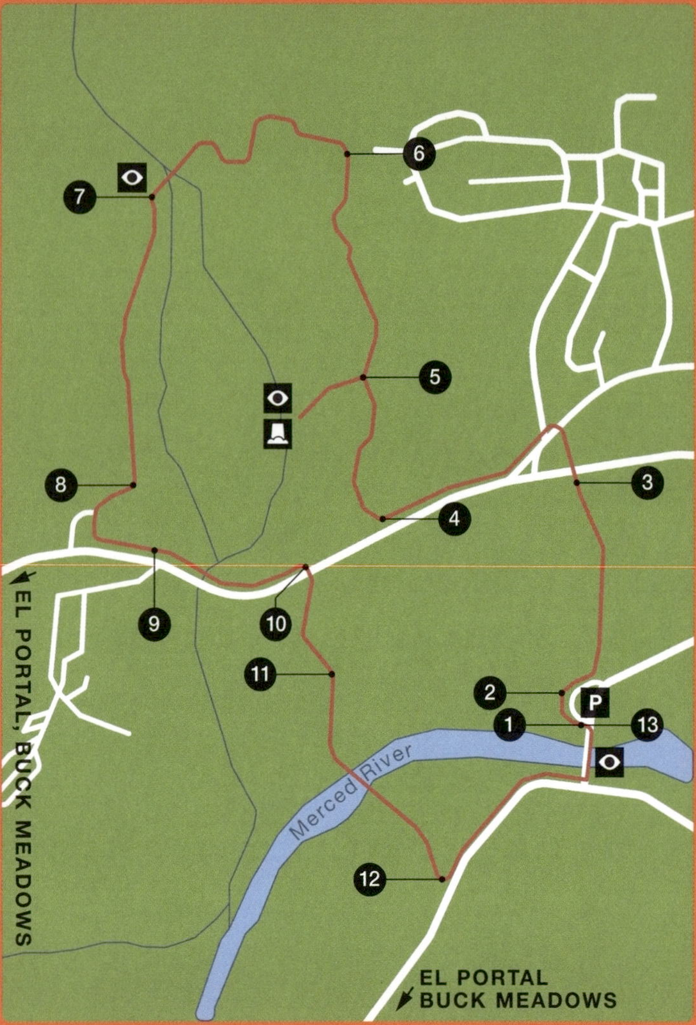

1
2
3
4
5
6
7
8
9
10
11
12
13
P
Merced River
EL PORTAL, BUCK MEADOWS
EL PORTAL
BUCK MEADOWS

P Parking · Viewpoint · Waterfall

ft
4500
4000
3500
3000
2500
2000
0.0
0.5
1.0
1.5
2.0
2.2 mi

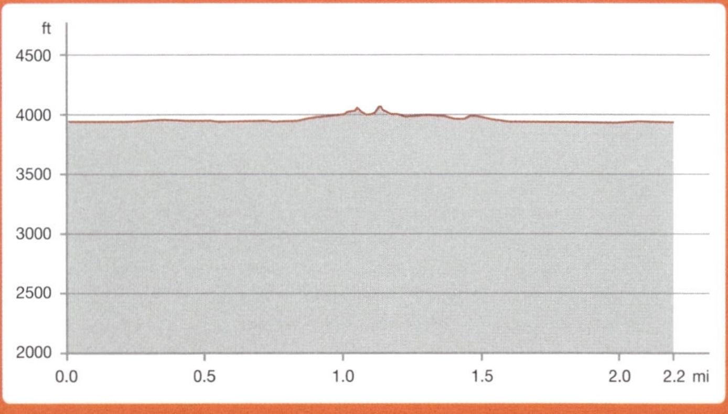

YOSEMITE VALLEY

EXPLORE YOSEMITE'S ICONIC VIEWPOINTS

YOSEMITE VALLEY, CA

22

LENGTH
2.2 miles (loop)

TIME & MONEY
1 hour, entrance fee

ELEVATION GAIN
125 feet

DIFFICULTY
Easy

CONDITIONS
Year-round; mostly exposed, icy areas in winter/ early spring

HIGHLIGHTS
Waterfalls, Half Dome views

ESSENTIALS

- **Find the trailhead:** From Oakdale, head northeast onto CA-120 east. In 25.0 miles, turn right to stay on CA-120 east. In 3.4 miles, turn right to stay on CA-120 east. In 40.7 miles, reach the Big Oak Flat Entrance and pay the park entrance fee. In 17.3 miles, turn left onto El Portal Road for Yosemite Valley. In 0.9 miles, El Portal Road turns slightly right and becomes Southside Drive. In 5.1 miles, turn left onto Sentinel Drive. The Sentinel Bridge parking lot is 200 feet ahead on your left. If the lot is full, you can park at Yosemite Village Parking and walk 0.2 miles to the trailhead. On the weekends from spring to fall, it's best to arrive before 8am to find parking and avoid extended delays. A timed-entry reservation may be required during peak season, so check online ahead of time and plan accordingly. Dogs are not allowed on the Yosemite Valley shuttles.
- **Land manager:** National Park Service (nps.gov/yose)

WHY YOU'LL LOVE IT

- Stunning Half Dome views
- Multiple vista points of Yosemite Falls
- Flat, paved trails are accessible for most dogs

Enjoy stunning views of Yosemite Falls and Half Dome as you meander through peaceful meadows in the heart of Yosemite Valley.

Each year, over four million visitors come to Yosemite National Park to see its famous granite cliffs and dramatic waterfalls. John Muir, a passionate wilderness advocate and writer, fell in love with Yosemite during his first visit in 1868. Throughout the 1870s and 1880s, he wrote about both Yosemite's beauty and humanity's destruction of the land. His publications and activism inspired Congress so much that in 1890, they took action to protect the area by making it America's third national park.

This introductory loop around Yosemite Valley brings you to some of the most popular sites in the valley, staying on mostly paved paths or boardwalks. Because the route stays within the populated valley, there are several entry and exit points along the loop, and it's one of the few hikes in the park that allows dogs.

From the Sentinel Bridge parking area, you'll head to Sentinel Bridge, where you'll discover a stunning vantage point of Half Dome. It's especially beautiful at sunrise or sunset—the soft light makes perfect reflections of Half Dome in the Merced River below. Half Dome is a 5,000-foot-tall granite formation and is one of Yosemite's most iconic landmarks. Hikers can get a permit to climb the rounded side of Half Dome using cables and wooden rungs bolted into the rock, but the permit system is competitive, and the hike is very strenuous.

After leaving Sentinel Bridge, you'll follow a boardwalk across Cook's Meadow, home to many animal species like monarch butterflies, deer, and chipmunks. If you're lucky, you may see rare animals like bobcats and black bears. There are seven different species of chipmunks in Yosemite. The most common is the Tahoe chipmunk, which has brighter and more contrasted coloration than any of the other chipmunk species. It's also the only local chipmunk species that climbs high in trees.

Along Cook's Meadow, you'll also see Lower and Upper Yosemite Falls in the distance—a hint at what's to come later in the hike. At 2,425 feet, Yosemite Falls is one of the tallest waterfalls in the United States. The first viewpoint on the Lower Yosemite Fall Trail is just under a quarter mile from Cook's Meadow. After another half mile, you'll reach a second vantage point. The waterfalls get their water from snowmelt in Yosemite Creek. During peak snowmelt in late spring, the flow can reach 2,400 gallons per second. You may get wet from the vantage point if you visit during this time. By late summer, however, this roaring springtime waterfall often turns to a small trickle.

Once you leave Yosemite Falls and head back to Cook's Meadow, you'll cross Superintendent's Bridge. In the center of the bridge, there's a tall marker showing different dates. The marker shows how high the Merced River rose during years of intense winter floods in the 1900s. The highest flood, in 1997, raised the water more than five feet above the bridge!

TURN-BY-TURN DIRECTIONS

1. From the Sentinel Bridge parking lot, walk 50 feet south to Sentinel Bridge for a view of Half Dome. When you're ready, head back to the parking lot.
2. At 300 feet, continue straight at the first unmarked junction, ignoring a trail on the left and curving around the parking lot. 100 feet ahead, turn left at the second unmarked junction onto the Cook's Meadow Trail.
3. At 0.3 miles, cross two roads (Northside Drive and Village Drive) with care—cars do not stop at these intersections. After crossing Village Drive, turn left to stay on the Cook's Meadow Trail and then stay left at the signpost for the pedestrian symbol toward Yosemite Falls.
4. At 0.4 miles, turn right at the junction marked for Lower Yosemite Fall. After 150 feet, stay right at the signposted junction for the Lower Yosemite Fall Trail.
5. At 0.6 miles, turn left at the junction marked for Falls View. The viewpoint is at the end of the short trail spur in 250 feet. Once you've enjoyed the view, turn back to the junction and continue on the Lower Yosemite Fall Trail.
6. At 1.0 miles, turn left at the junction marked for Lower Yosemite Fall.
7. At 1.2 miles, cross a bridge over Yosemite Creek and then reach the Lower Yosemite Fall Vista Point. When you're ready, continue on the Lower Yosemite Fall Trail.
8. At 1.4 miles, turn right at the unmarked junction to continue on the Lower Yosemite Fall Trail. After 200 feet, keep left at the signposted junction for Yosemite Lodge. After another 100 feet, turn left at the signposted junction to continue on the Lower Yosemite Fall Trail—do not cross Northside Drive.
9. At 1.5 miles, continue straight, passing the marked junction for the restrooms on your left. After 50 feet, continue straight at the unmarked junction—do not turn left.
10. At 1.7 miles, turn right at the unmarked junction before the Yosemite Falls bus stop to cross the road (Northside Drive) with care—cars do not stop. After crossing the road, you're back on the Cook's Meadow Trail.
11. At 1.8 miles, turn right at the unmarked junction toward the Superintendent's bridge.
12. At 2.0 miles, turn left at the unmarked junction to head back to Sentinel Bridge—do not cross the road.
13. At 2.1 miles, turn left to cross Sentinel Bridge and arrive back at the parking lot.

MARIPOSA
GROVELAND

P

1

2

3

4

Grizzly Peak

P Parking

Mountain

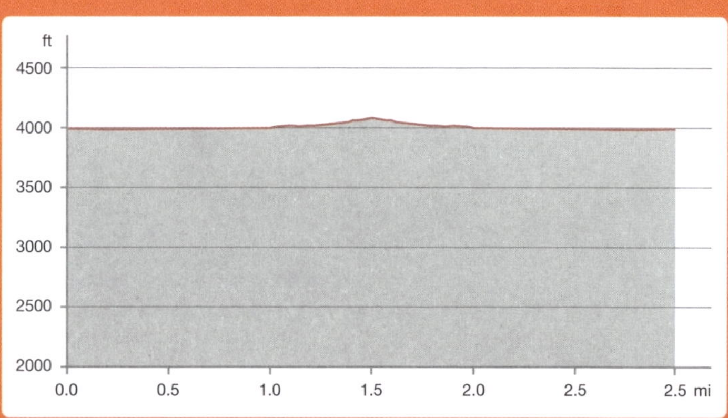

MIRROR LAKE

AN ACCESSIBLE LAKE IN YOSEMITE VALLEY

YOSEMITE VALLEY, CA

23

LENGTH
2.5 miles
(round trip)

TIME & MONEY
1 hour 15 min.,
entrance fee

ELEVATION GAIN
110 feet

DIFFICULTY
Easy

CONDITIONS
Year-round;
partially shaded,
icy areas in winter/
early spring

HIGHLIGHTS
Seasonal lake

ESSENTIALS

- **Find the trailhead:** From the Yosemite National Park Big Oak Flat Entrance, enter the park and continue for 17.3 miles. Turn left onto El Portal Road for Yosemite Valley. In 0.9 miles, El Portal Road turns slightly right and becomes Southside Drive. In 6.1 miles, turn right onto Curry Village Drive. In 0.3 miles, follow Curry Village Drive to the right as it turns into Happy Isles Loop Road. Parking is available on the side of Happy Isles Loop Road. Parking in Yosemite Valley is limited—on the weekends from spring to fall, it's best to arrive before 8am to avoid extended delays. Dogs are not allowed on the Yosemite Valley shuttles.
- **Land manager:** National Park Service (nps.gov/yose)

WHY YOU'LL LOVE IT

- Flat, paved trail is accessible for most dogs
- Reflections of Half Dome and Mount Watkins on the lake
- Swimming in the lake (permitted for humans only)

Wind upstream alongside Tenaya Creek on a pine-shaded, paved trail to Mirror Lake.

You'll begin your hike on the easternmost side of Yosemite Valley in the Curry Village area. David and Jennie Curry, both former teachers, started Curry Village in 1899. They wanted to offer visitors an affordable option to stay in Yosemite as opposed to the expensive hotels. As you walk along Happy Isles Loop Road, you'll see Lower Pines Campground on one side and Upper Pines Campground on the other. Lower Pines is only open seasonally, while Upper Pines is open year-round.

Less than a quarter mile into your hike, you'll cross the Merced River, which flows through the heart of Yosemite Valley. Native Americans have lived in Yosemite for approximately 4,000 years. They called Yosemite Valley "Ahwahnee" (meaning "gaping mouth-like place"). By the late 1700s, the primary tribe in Yosemite was the Southern Sierra Miwok. They built their villages by the river for easy access to fishing. They lived in homes called "umachas," which are cone-like structures made from incense cedar trees. In the mid 1800s, California Gold Rush miners and tourists started forcing themselves onto Native American land. A group called the Mariposa Battalion led multiple campaigns to kill the Ahwahneechee people and destroy their villages, which included the forced removal of Chief Tenaya. As a result, the Native population declined significantly in the following decades. The Native Americans faced a diminishing number of sustainable options for living in Yosemite, and the National Park Service destroyed the last Native American home in 1969.

After crossing the Merced River, you'll continue your hike on a wide, paved trail that's open to bikes, strollers, and sometimes cars. The trail is partially shaded with pine and oak trees. You may see acorns on the ground and bright-green moss on tree bark or rocks. Unlike most plants, moss absorbs water and nutrients through its surface instead of its roots, allowing it to grow on surfaces that appear inhospitable.

About a mile into the hike, you'll reach Mirror Lake. Though called a lake, it now resembles more of a pool—each year, more sediment collects in the pool, reducing the water Tenaya Creek sends to Mirror Lake. The lake's size changes each year based on recent rainfall and the season you visit. In the early spring, the lake is usually full. But by late summer, it often shrinks to a small pool or disappears completely. Although dogs are not allowed, you can swim in most bodies of water in the park. Besides swimming in Mirror Lake, you can also swim in the Merced River, provided you enter from a sandy beach. Yosemite Search and Rescue saves over 15 people each year from the park's waters, so make sure to learn about water safety before you swim.

TURN-BY-TURN DIRECTIONS

1. From the parking area, turn left onto Happy Isles Loop Road.
2. At 0.2 miles, continue straight past the Service Vehicles sign. After 50 feet, continue straight and pass a sign for Mirror Lake.
3. At 0.5 miles, turn left at the signpost for Mirror Lake. Stay on the paved trail until you reach Mirror Lake, ignoring the dirt Mirror Lake Trail that runs parallel. Dogs are not allowed on Mirror Lake Trail.
4. At 1.2 miles, reach Mirror Lake. There are restrooms and trash bins here. When you're ready, retrace your steps back to the parking area.

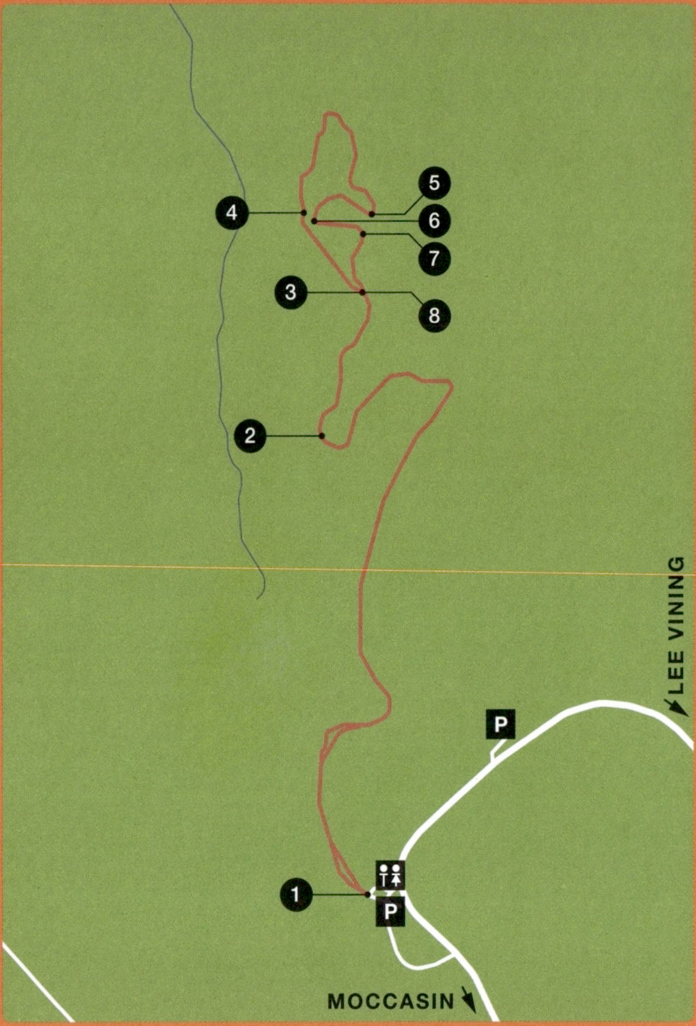

4
5
6
7
3
8
2
1
LEE VINING
P
MOCCASIN

P Parking
Toilet

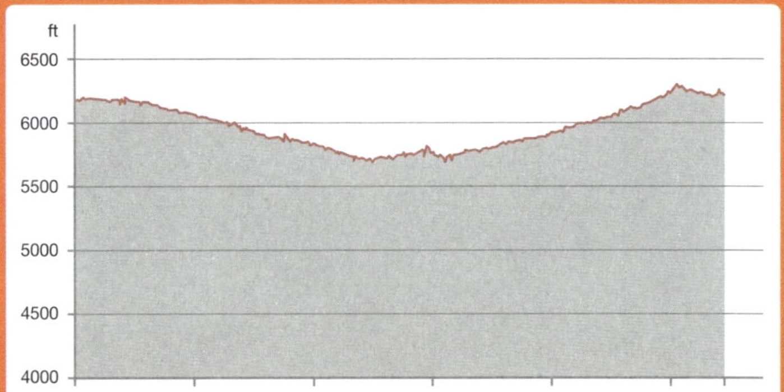

TUOLUMNE GROVE

GIANT SEQUOIAS IN YOSEMITE

TUOLUMNE MEADOWS, CA

24

LENGTH
2.7 miles
(lollipop loop)

TIME & MONEY
1 hour 15 min.,
entrance fee

ELEVATION GAIN
497 feet

DIFFICULTY
Easy

CONDITIONS
Year-round;
partially shaded,
icy in winter/early
spring

HIGHLIGHTS
Giant sequoias,
tunnel tree

ESSENTIALS

- **Find the trailhead:** From the Big Oak Flat Entrance, pay the park entrance fee and then continue into the park. In 7.7 miles, turn left onto Tioga Road. In 0.6 miles, turn left into the parking lot. Tioga Road closes in the winter past the Tuolumne Grove entrance. The parking lot is accessible year-round.
- **Land manager:** National Park Service (nps.gov/yose)

WHY YOU'LL LOVE IT

- Wide, paved trail will be accessible for most dogs
- Giant sequoia grove
- Walk through a tree tunnel

Discover towering giant sequoias and explore two fallen sequoias in Yosemite's peaceful Tuolumne Grove.

Around two dozen mature giant sequoias live in Tuolumne Grove. Giant sequoias are the largest tree species in the world and one of the oldest too—the oldest known giant sequoias are over 3,200 years old! These majestic trees can grow to over 250 feet tall, with trunks of over 30 feet in diameter. In comparison to the related coastal redwoods, giant sequoias have wider trunks and usually grow in the Sierra Nevada mountains.

Your hike starts on the Old Big Oak Flat Road, which was one of the first roads that took western explorers into Yosemite Valley by stagecoach or car. Today, this section of the road is only open to hikers. In the winter, snow and ice may cover the trail and make the hike slippery.

As you descend into the grove, keep an eye out for birds such as Steller's jays or western tanagers flying among the sugar pine and white fir trees. Western tanagers are songbirds with bright-yellow bodies, reddish-orange heads, and black feathers. In the spring and summer, you might hear these birds singing to establish territory or attract mates. They have a short, two- to three-note song that usually lasts around two and a half seconds.

Around one mile into the hike, you'll find picnic tables and a sign signaling the start of the Tuolumne Grove Loop. Your first stop along the loop is a small bridge crossing North Crane Creek. As you walk to the back of the grove, you'll see informational displays about the giant sequoias. The highlight of this loop is two trees that you can walk through. First, you'll find a fallen tree a couple feet past the informational display on "Shallow Root Systems." You can explore the inside of the tree and beautiful root system as you walk through its entire length.

Your last stop on the Tuolumne Grove Loop is over another small bridge. This takes you to the second and more famous Dead Giant Tunnel Tree. The Dead Giant was the first tunnel tree ever created in the Sierra Nevada. It came before the more famous Wawona Tree in Mariposa Grove that fell in 1969. In 1878, the owners of Tuolumne Grove hollowed out a dead sequoia tree to attract more visitors—including former New York Governor Al Smith. Their strategy worked then and continues to draw tourists today. Standing in the middle of the 29.5-foot-wide stump gives you perspective on how big the giant sequoias are.

TURN-BY-TURN DIRECTIONS

1. From the trailhead on the west side of the parking lot, head straight onto the Old Big Oak Flat Road.
2. At 0.9 miles, reach a "Welcome to Tuolumne Grove" sign. Continue straight to the junction for the Tuolumne Grove Loop.
3. At 1.1 miles, stay left to start the Tuolumne Grove Loop clockwise.
4. At 1.2 miles, pass a picnic table to your right and turn left at the junction marked "Begin Grove Loop."
5. At 1.4 miles, explore a fallen tree next to the sign marked "Shallow Root Systems."
6. At 1.5 miles, turn left at the junction marked "Tunnel Tree & Exit."
7. At 1.6 miles, walk through the Dead Giant Tunnel Tree.
8. At 1.7 miles, finish the loop and turn left at the marked junction to retrace your steps back to the parking lot.

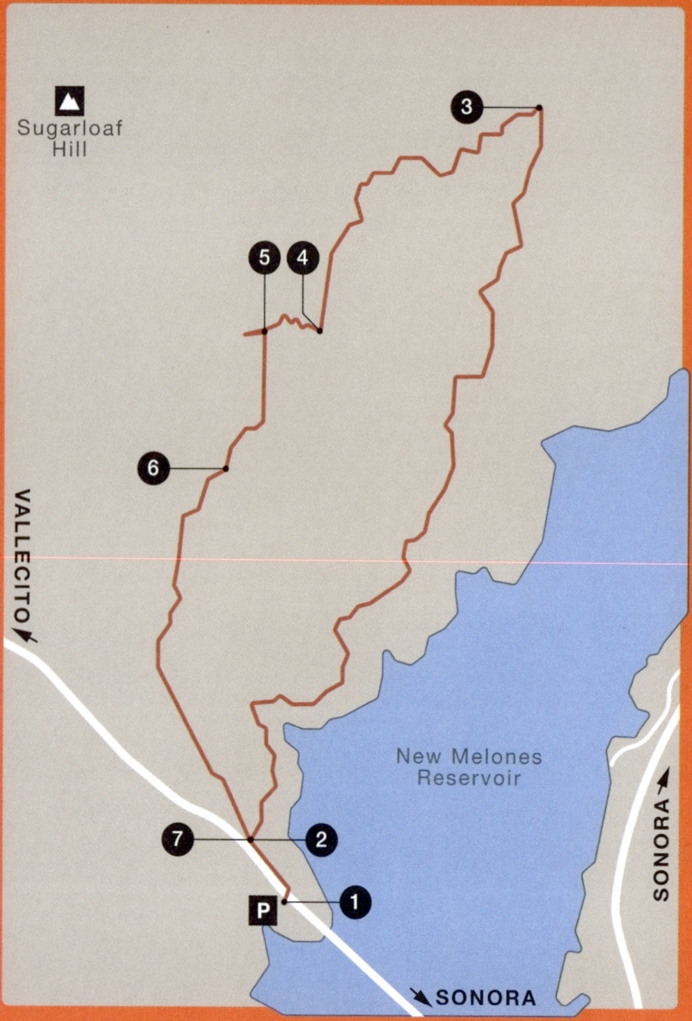

Sugarloaf Hill
VALLECITO
New Melones Reservoir
SONORA
SONORA
P
1
2
3
4
5
6
7

P Parking   Mountain

ft
2500
2000
1500
1000
500
0
0.0
0.5
1.0
1.5
2.0
2.5
3.0
3.4 mi

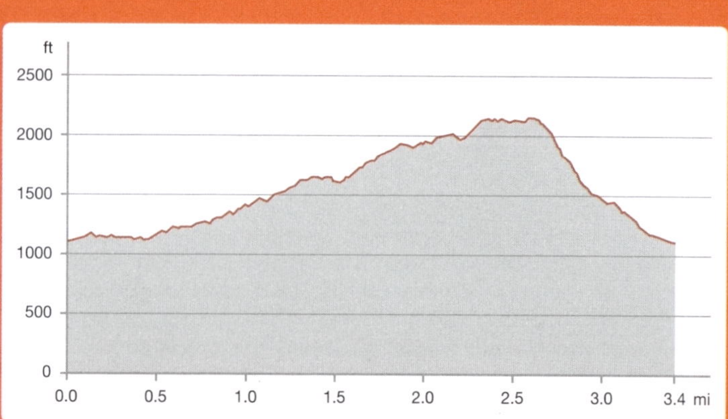

DUCHESS MINE TRAIL

HISTORIC RUINS AND RESERVOIR VIEWS

ANGELS CAMP, CA

25

LENGTH
3.4 miles (loop)

TIME & MONEY
2 hours, free

ELEVATION GAIN
1,340 feet

DIFFICULTY
Easy

CONDITIONS
Year-round; exposed

HIGHLIGHTS
Reservoir views, historic ruins

ESSENTIALS

- **Find the trailhead:** From downtown Stockton, merge onto CA-4 east. In 1.9 miles, take the exit for CA-99 south/CA-4 east toward Fresno. In 0.6 miles, take the exit for Golden Gate Avenue. After 0.3 miles, turn left onto CA-4 east/South Golden Gate Avenue. In 0.5 miles, turn left onto CA-4 east and continue for 51.0 miles. Turn right onto Parrotts Ferry Road. After 4.9 miles, just before you reach the bridge, the parking lot will be on your right.

- **Land manager:** Bureau of Land Management (blm.gov)

WHY YOU'LL LOVE IT

- Stunning views of New Melones Reservoir and Parrott's Ferry Bridge
- Abandoned vehicles
- Graffitied military structure

Climb to an expansive plateau overlooking New Melones Reservoir. Along the way, explore abandoned cars and a painted military relic.

You'll start your hike on the Duchess Mine Trail by meandering along New Melones Reservoir. As soon as you get on the trail, you'll have views of the reservoir and Parrott's Ferry Bridge. In 1860, Thomas H. Parrott built a ferry crossing to connect the mining towns of Tuttletown and Vallecito. The ferry operated until 1903, when it was converted to a bridge. Although Parrot's Ferry Bridge is mostly either gone or under water, the location is still recognized as a California Historical Landmark.

In the spring and early summer, you may see various species of wildflowers along the narrow dirt trail. When the flowers bloom, you'll see white and purple flowers from California yerba santa, red flowers from Indian paintbrush, orange flowers from sticky monkey flower, and yellow flowers from yellow yarrow.

The hike is historically named after Duchess Mine, a hard-rock gold mine, but you won't see any remnants of the mine on this trail. Instead, about a mile in, roughly 30 feet into the bushes to your right, look for an abandoned car. After another quarter mile, you'll see two, more visible abandoned cars closer to the trail. Given the structure of the cars, they were likely brought after the original Gold Rush.

As you move away from the reservoir, you'll start ascending to an expansive plateau. The plateau stretches about 1,500 feet from end to end, offering wide open views. At the top, you'll see a distinctive military relic painted like a butterfly. Some believe that the relic looks like a torpedo-looking bomb, which has earned the trail its nickname as the "Bomb Trail." The structure is most likely a transducer sonar from the Navy, though it's unclear when or why it was left here.

After the plateau, you'll start your descent back down to the parking lot. The descent is steep and rocky. If you prefer to have a gentler descent, hike the Duchess Mine Trail clockwise, instead of counter-clockwise. Most of the Duchess Mine Trail is exposed, and the direct sun can be hotter than the temperature suggests. Start your hike early if you hike in the summer and bring plenty of water.

TURN-BY-TURN DIRECTIONS

1. From the parking lot, cross the road with care. Cars do not stop. After 200 feet, you'll see a small trail marker on your left. Continue straight at this marker.
2. At 0.1 miles, pass between two large boulders to reach the start of the Duchess Mine Trail. Take the trail to your right to begin the loop counter-clockwise.
3. At 1.5 miles, stay on the unmarked Duchess Mine Trail, which curves left.
4. At 2.2 miles, take a sharp right at the unmarked junction.
5. At 2.3 miles, turn right at the unmarked junction onto a narrow trail. Explore the graffitied structure 150 feet ahead. When you're ready, come back to this junction and turn right to continue the hike.
6. At 2.6 miles, there's a view of the reservoir on your left. Turn right at the unmarked junction.
7. At 3.2 miles, arrive at the junction from Step 2. Retrace your steps back to the parking lot. There are no facilities at the parking lot, so be sure to pack essentials for your dog.

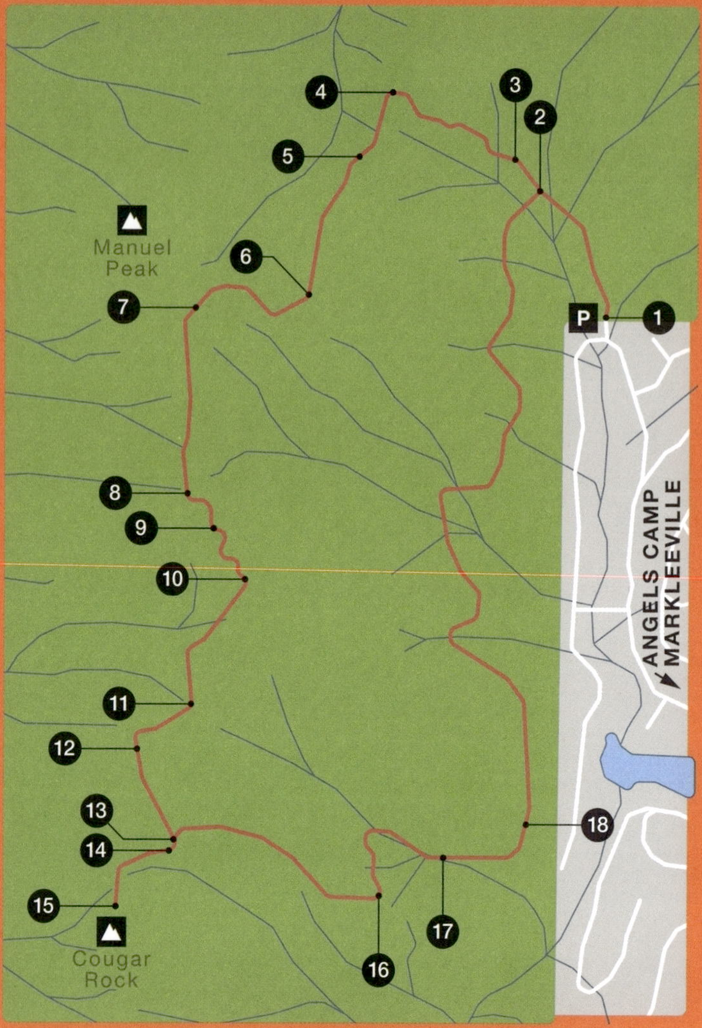

Manuel Peak
Cougar Rock
ANGELS CAMP
MARKLEEVILLE
P
1
2
3
4
5
6
7
8
9
10
11
12
13
14
15
16
17
18

P Parking

Mountain

ft
5000
4500
4000
3500
3000
2500
0.0
0.5
1.0
1.5
2.0
2.5
3.0
3.5
4.0
4.4
mi

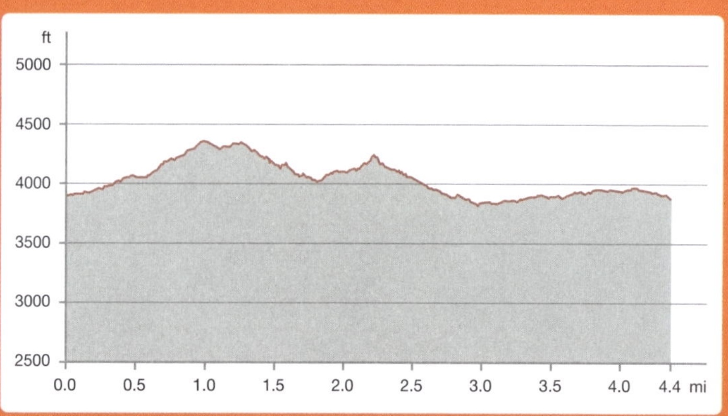

ARNOLD RIM TRAIL

SUMMIT VIEWS AND A SCENIC OUTCROP

ARNOLD, CA

26

LENGTH
4.4 miles (loop)

TIME & MONEY
2 hours 15 min., free

ELEVATION GAIN
666 feet

DIFFICULTY
Moderate

CONDITIONS
Year-round; mostly exposed

HIGHLIGHTS
Mountain vistas, rocky overlook

ESSENTIALS

- **Find the trailhead:** From downtown Stockton, get onto CA-4 east. In 1.9 miles, take the exit toward Fresno and then merge onto CA-99 south/CA-4 east. In 0.5 miles, take the exit for CA-4/CA-99 south and proceed for 0.6 miles. Take the exit for Golden Gate Avenue, and in 0.3 miles, turn left onto CA-4/South Golden Gate Avenue. After 0.5 miles, turn left onto CA-4 east and continue for 64.5 miles. Turn left onto Lakemont Drive. In 1.1 miles, Lakemont Drive splits into a fork. Take the right fork and park on the side of the road on Lakemont Drive. There are no facilities available.
- **Land manager:** U.S. Forest Service (fs.usda.gov)

WHY YOU'LL LOVE IT

- Mountain views from the Top of the World vista point
- Scenic overlook at Cougar Rock
- Less crowded section of the Arnold Rim Trail

Hike to the Top of the World and Cougar Rock overlook for sweeping views spanning from Mt. Diablo to snowy Sierra peaks.

The Arnold Rim Trail is a 23-mile multi-use trail system that winds through the Stanislaus National Forest in the central Sierra Nevada Mountains. Stanislaus National Forest is one of the oldest national forests in the U.S. (established in 1897). It gets its name from the Stanislaus River, a 150-mile waterway. Stanislaus comes from Estanislao, leader of the Lakisamni tribe who led a revolt against the Mexican government. His knowledge of Spanish and Mexican military tactics helped his army have initial success on the battlefield. He organized a resistance that defeated several Mexican military expeditions in 1828, but he was overpowered in 1829.

The trailhead starts in a quiet residential area. You'll access the Arnold Rim Trail via a wide fire trail beginning at Lakemont Drive. After around a quarter mile, you'll turn onto a forest service road and begin climbing. Along the trail, you'll pass various plants such as wavy strap-leafed California soaproot and fern-like mountain misery. Native American tribes mixed crushed soaproot bulbs with water to create soap, and the Miwok people referred to mountain misery as "kit-kit-dizze" and used it for medicinal purposes—they brewed tea from the leaves to treat colds, coughs, and other ailments.

Around a mile in, you'll reach the Top of the World. On a clear day, you'll have panoramic views that stretch from Mt. Diablo in the East Bay to snow-capped Sierra peaks. In late spring and early summer, you might see pale swallowtail butterflies flying around, which have black and cream coloring with wingspans of around 5 inches. They are among California's largest native butterflies.

After the Top of the World, you'll descend back below the treeline. This section of the hike provides a shaded break for you and your dogs for a little over a half mile until you reach Cougar Rock. You'll need to do some short scrambling to get around the rock for a view. The scramble should be accessible for most dogs. From Cougar Rock, you'll enjoy sweeping westward views across the Central Valley toward the Coast Ranges.

The hike returns to the trailhead via a forest service road. Although there's not much activity on the service road, the wide road is a comfortable walk for the dogs. Much of the California wilderness is in mountain lion country, and hikers have reported seeing mountain lions on the Arnold Rim Trail. Although it can be tempting to take your dog off-leash, leashing them will best protect them from rare mountain lion attacks.

TURN-BY-TURN DIRECTIONS

1. From the unmarked trailhead, pass the iron gate and continue straight on the obvious trail.
2. At 0.2 miles, turn right at the unmarked junction to start the counter-clockwise loop.
3. At 0.3 miles, turn left at the junction marked as "5N49."
4. At 0.4 miles, turn left at the "LMP #01" signpost. After 50 feet, continue straight at the signposted junction for the Arnold Rim Trail Alternate Route, ignoring the trail on the right.
5. At 0.6 miles, stay right at the signposted fork to continue on the Arnold Rim Trail Alternate Route toward Top of the World.
6. At 0.8 miles, turn right at the signposted fork to continue on the Arnold Rim Trail Alternate Route.
7. At 1.0 miles, turn left at the signposted junction onto the Arnold Rim Trail toward Top of the World.
8. At 1.2 miles, reach the Top of the World. When you're ready, continue straight.
9. At 1.3 miles, stay right at the signposted fork to stay on the Arnold Rim Trail. The next 0.3 miles have signposts reminding you to not cut switchbacks.
10. At 1.6 miles, turn right at the signposted junction to continue on the Arnold Rim Trail.
11. At 1.8 miles, turn right at the signposted junction to continue on the Arnold Rim Trail toward Cougar Rock.
12. At 1.9 miles, turn left at the signposted junction to continue on the Arnold Rim Trail.
13. At 2.0 miles, continue straight at the signposted junction to continue on the Arnold Rim Trail. After 100 feet, turn right at the signposted junction to Cougar Rock, 0.2 miles ahead. You'll come back to this step after Cougar Rock.
14. At 2.1 miles, continue straight at the signposted junction to Cougar Rock.
15. At 2.2 miles, turn right at the signposted junction to Cougar Rock. After 500 feet, arrive at Cougar Rock. When you're ready, return to the junction from Step 13 and turn right onto the Sunset Loop Trail.
16. At 2.7 miles, turn left at the signposted junction onto U.S. Forest Service Road 4N36.
17. At 2.9 miles, turn left at the junction marked "5N95Y."
18. At 4.1 miles, arrive back to the junction from Step 2. Retrace your steps back to the trailhead.

LAKE TAHOE AND DESOLATION WILDERNESS

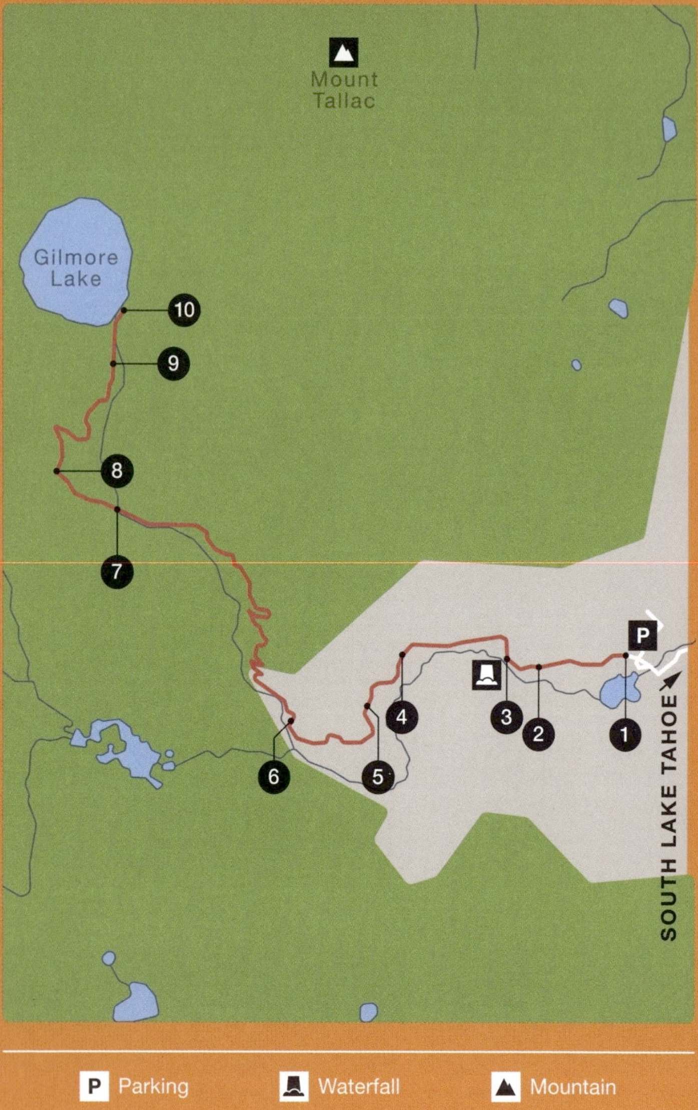

Mount Tallac
Gilmore Lake
10
9
8
7
6
5
4
3
2
1
P
SOUTH LAKE TAHOE
P Parking
Waterfall
Mountain

ft
8500
8000
7500
7000
6500
6000
0.0 0.5 1.0 1.5 2.0 2.5 3.0 3.5 4.0 4.5 5.0 5.5 6.0 6.5 7.0 7.5 8.0 8.3 mi

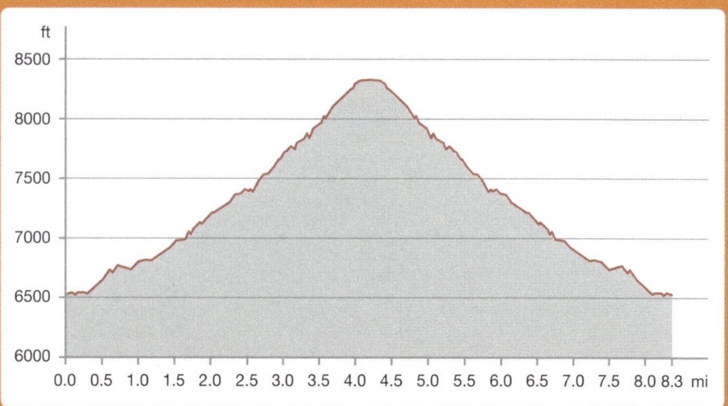

GILMORE LAKE

HIKE TO A PRISTINE ALPINE LAKE

SOUTH LAKE TAHOE, CA

27

LENGTH
8.3 miles
(round trip)

TIME & MONEY
4 hours, free

ELEVATION GAIN
1,978 feet

DIFFICULTY
Strenuous

CONDITIONS
May–October; partially exposed, seasonal closures in the winter

HIGHLIGHTS
Alpine lake, mountain views, historic resort

ESSENTIALS

- **Find the trailhead:** From downtown Sacramento, head south on 9th Street. In 1.0 miles, turn left onto X Street. After 400 feet, stay in the middle lane to take the US-50 east ramp and then merge onto US-50 east in 0.3 miles. Continue for 93.4 miles. At North Upper Truckee Road, turn left. In 2.3 miles, turn left onto Lake Tahoe Boulevard. In 1.3 miles, turn left onto Tahoe Mountain Road. After 1.1 miles, turn right onto Glenmore Way. In 109 feet, turn left onto Dundee Circle and then follow the road left to stay on Dundee Circle. Dundee Circle becomes Tahoe Mountain Road in 200 feet. In 0.5 miles, turn left onto Fallen Leaf Road and proceed for 2.8 miles. Continue straight as the road turns into Glen Alpine Road. In 0.6 miles, the road dead ends into the parking lot, where there are restrooms and trash bins. There is no potable water, so you'll need to pack your own.

- **Land manager:** U.S. Forest Service (fs.usda.gov)

WHY YOU'LL LOVE IT

- Granite peaks in the Sierra Nevada wilderness
- Various water sources for your dogs to play in
- You can extend the hike to other alpine lakes

Journey through the Desolation Wilderness and past the historic Glen Alpine Springs resort to reach Gilmore Lake.

The Glen Alpine Trailhead is a primary access point to the Desolation Wilderness, one of Northern California's most treasured wilderness areas for its pristine alpine lakes and granite landscapes. From the Glen Alpine Trail, hikers can reach several alpine lakes such as Grass Lake, Gilmore Lake, and Lake Aloha, as well as the summit of Mount Tallac. Dogs are allowed throughout the Desolation Wilderness.

The trail starts on Glen Alpine Spring Road, a wide, rocky road that cars once used to get to the Glen Alpine Springs resort. In late spring and early summer, snowmelt can flood this section of the trail—the trail is still passable, but your feet may get wet. Around half a mile in, you'll see the 50-foot Modjeska Falls on your left. The falls are particularly stunning in late spring and early summer when the water levels are high. After the falls, you'll cross a small footbridge before arriving at the historic Glen Alpine Springs resort.

Built by Nathan Gilmore in the mid-1800s, this was one of Lake Tahoe's first tourist resorts. Gilmore marketed the resort to San Francisco residents who wanted to spend their summer in nature. He also sold the natural spring water as "Glen Alpine Tonic Water." In the late 1900s, a holding company purchased Glen Alpine Springs after the previous owners passed. They neglected the resort for years before Robert Fritschi purchased it and restored many of the buildings. Interpretive displays throughout the resort were installed by the nonprofit Historical Preservation of Glen Alpine Springs, which maintains the site through volunteer efforts and donations.

After you leave Glen Alpine Springs, you'll continue to climb up the rocky trail until you reach a clearing in the trees with views of granite peaks. From here, you'll start a series of switchbacks up rocky terrain. After the switchbacks, there are a few stream crossings where your dog can cool off. The crossings are generally straightforward, but they can be a little tricky in the late spring and early summer if there is high snow runoff.

Around three and a half miles into the hike, you'll join the famous Pacific Crest Trail. Seventeen miles of the Pacific Crest Trail run through the Desolation Wilderness, connecting major destinations like Lake Aloha and Gilmore Lake. Because the last half mile goes above 8,000 feet in elevation, snow can cover the trails until mid-June. Once you arrive at Gilmore Lake, you can explore the shoreline with your dog before heading back the way you came.

TURN-BY-TURN DIRECTIONS

1. The trail starts at the west end of the Glen Alpine parking area, past the green gate.
2. At 0.3 miles, keep right at the signposted fork to continue on Glen Alpine Springs Road.
3. At 0.5 miles, pass Modjeska Falls on your left. When you're ready, continue straight. In 500 feet, continue straight at the signposted junction, ignoring the fork on your right.
4. At 1.1 miles, enter the historic preservation of Glen Alpine Springs. Continue straight; don't turn onto any of the side roads in the resort.
5. At 1.2 miles, continue straight at the signposted junction for Susie Lake and Grass Lake. You're now on the Glen Alpine Trail.
6. At 1.7 miles, continue straight at the signposted junction, ignoring the trail on the left for Grass Lake. If you want to extend your hike, you can add an additional mile (each way, two miles total) to Grass Lake and continue to Gilmore Lake from this junction.
7. At 3.4 miles, turn right at the signposted junction for Gilmore Lake.
8. At 3.6 miles, turn right at the signposted junction onto the Pacific Crest Trail toward Gilmore Lake.
9. At 3.8 miles, continue straight at the signposted junction onto the Mount Tallac Trail, ignoring the Pacific Crest Trail that continues left.
10. At 4.2 miles, arrive at Gilmore Lake. When you're ready, retrace your steps back to the parking lot.

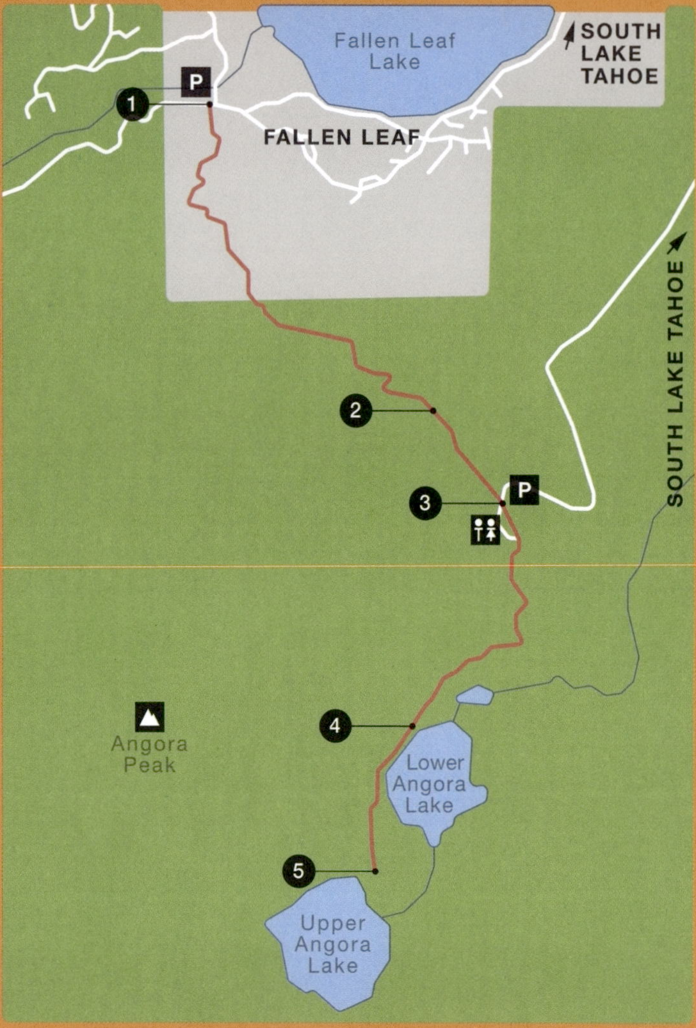

Fallen Leaf Lake
SOUTH LAKE TAHOE
P
1
FALLEN LEAF
2
3
P
SOUTH LAKE TAHOE
4
Angora Peak
Lower Angora Lake
5
Upper Angora Lake

P Parking Toilet Mountain

ft
8000
7500
7000
6500
6000
5500
0.0
0.5
1.0
1.5
2.0
2.5
3.0
3.4 mi

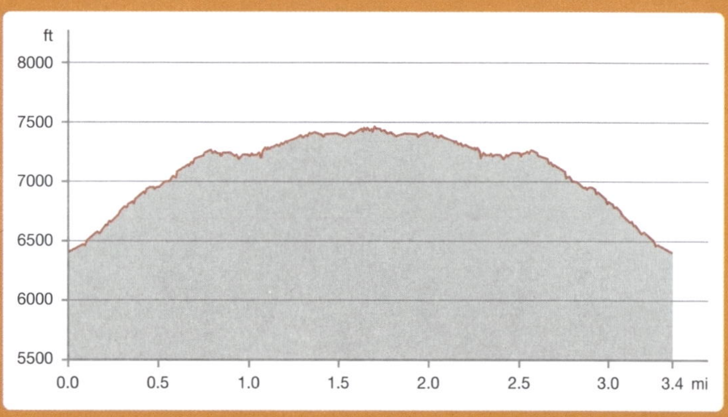

ANGORA LAKES

ALPINE LAKES NEAR A SEASONAL RESORT

SOUTH LAKE TAHOE, CA

28

LENGTH
3.4 miles
(round trip)

TIME & MONEY
2 hours, free

ELEVATION GAIN
1,000 feet

DIFFICULTY
Moderate

CONDITIONS
May–October; mostly exposed, subject to seasonal closures in the winter

HIGHLIGHTS
Alpine lakes, lakeside resort

ESSENTIALS

- **Find the trailhead:** From the Heavenly Village in South Lake Tahoe, head west on Lake Tahoe Boulevard. In 4.7 miles, continue straight to stay on Lake Tahoe Boulevard. After 2.5 miles, turn right onto Tahoe Mountain Road and continue for 1.1 miles. At Glenmore Way, turn right. In 109 feet, turn left onto Dundee Circle and follow the road left to stay on Dundee Circle. Dundee Circle becomes Tahoe Mountain Road in 200 feet. In 0.5 miles, turn left onto Fallen Leaf Road. In 2.8 miles, the parking area is on your right, across from the Fallen Leaf Fire Station. The parking area does not have any facilities.
- **Land manager:** U.S. Forest Service (fs.usda.gov)

WHY YOU'LL LOVE IT

- Alpine lakes just 1.5 miles away
- Resort has snacks for sale in summer

Take a short climb to Lower and Upper Angora Lakes, nestled beneath granite peaks. In the summer, enjoy Angora Lakes Resort's famous lemonade from the lakeside snack bar.

Perched at 7,450 feet, the Angora Lakes lie in granite bowls beneath Angora and Echo Peaks. In the late 1800s, Nathan Gilmore brought Angora goats to graze in the Fallen Leaf area, leading to naming the lakes and peak after them. This is the same Nathan Gilmore who built the Glen Alpine Springs resort from the Gilmore Lake chapter. Although no Angora goats live in the area today, Lower and Upper Angora Lakes and Angora Peak still kept their names.

You'll begin your adventure from the Fallen Leaf Fire Station. As you climb the rocky switchbacks of the Angora Lakes Trail, Lake Tahoe comes into view through gaps in the forest canopy. After around a quarter of a mile, the terrain shifts from rock to dirt. In the early summer, running water from the season's snowmelt can make this section muddy, but still passable.

As you climb toward Lower and Upper Angora Lakes, you'll pass through mixed forests dominated by western white pine and California incense cedar, both of which can grow to more than 100 feet tall. Western white pine has needles bundled in groups of five, while California incense cedar has scale-like leaves with a pleasant aromatic bark. Below the canopy, pinemat manzanita carpets the forest floor alongside abundant new growth—evidence of the forest's recovery from the devastating 2007 Angora Fire. The fire consumed over 3,100 acres, destroyed over 240 homes, and prompted over 2,100 heroic firefighters to battle the blaze for 8 days.

Beyond the Angora Lake parking lot, the trail opens into more spacious terrain dotted with large granite boulders. Around a mile and a half into the hike, you'll reach Lower Angora Lake. Of the two lakes, Lower Angora offers the quieter, more subdued scenery. The flat shoreline makes it easy for you and your dog to access the water.

Less than a ten-minute walk beyond Lower Angora Lake, you'll arrive at Angora Lakes Resort, which has been operating since the 1920s. The intimate resort sits on the shore of Upper Angora Lake, where you'll enjoy the scenery of towering granite cliffs rising behind its chilly waters. The lake's mirror-like surface reflects the dramatic rock faces and snow-dusted peaks. When the resort is open for the season, you'll see a sign that tells visitors to leash dogs when others are present. You can buy the resort's famous lemonade (cash preferred) and sit by the lake while taking in one of the Sierra Nevada's most accessible and rewarding alpine lake hikes.

TURN-BY-TURN DIRECTIONS

1. The trail starts next to the Fallen Leaf Fire Station. Head onto the Angora Lakes Trail at the signpost.
2. At 0.8 miles, continue straight, ignoring the signpost on your right for the Lily Lake Trail.
3. At 1.0 miles, turn right on the unmarked road to the Angora Lakes Resort parking lot, where there are trash bins and restrooms. Continue straight through the parking lot to connect to Angora Ridge Road.
4. At 1.4 miles, reach Lower Angora Lake. There are multiple spots to enter the lake on your left.
5. At 1.7 miles, arrive at Angora Lakes Resort. Turn right at the signpost for the beach and walk another 200 feet, past the snack bar, to reach the lakeshore. When you're ready, retrace your steps back to the parking lot.

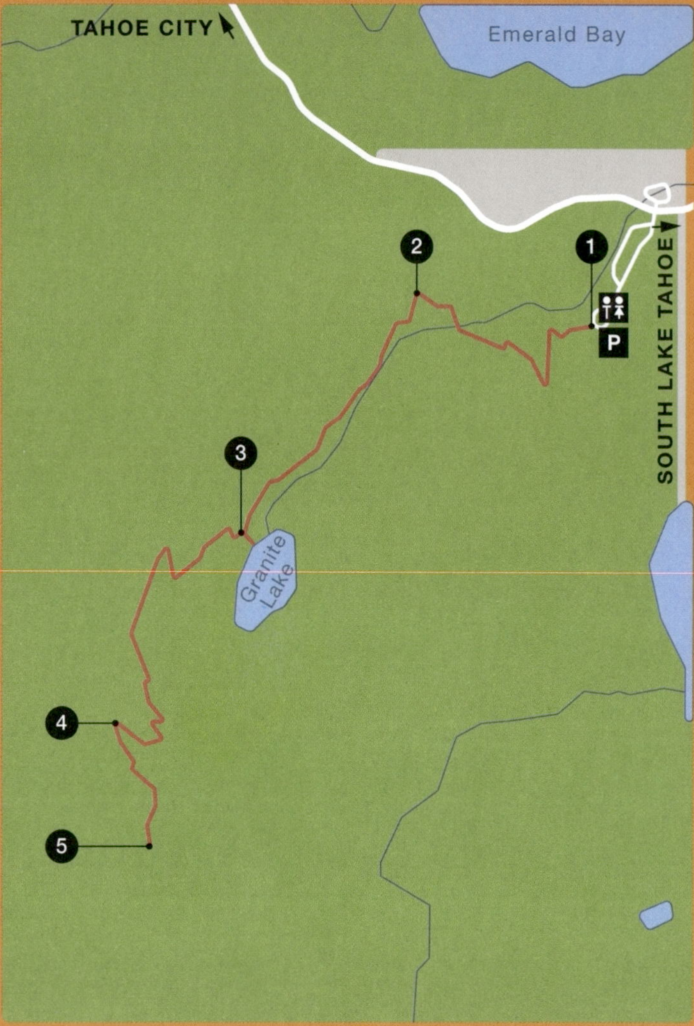

TAHOE CITY
Emerald Bay
SOUTH LAKE TAHOE
Granite Lake
1
2
3
4
5
P

P Parking   Toilet

ft
9000
8500
8000
7500
7000
6500
0.0
0.5
1.0
1.5
2.0
2.5
3.0
3.5
4.1 mi

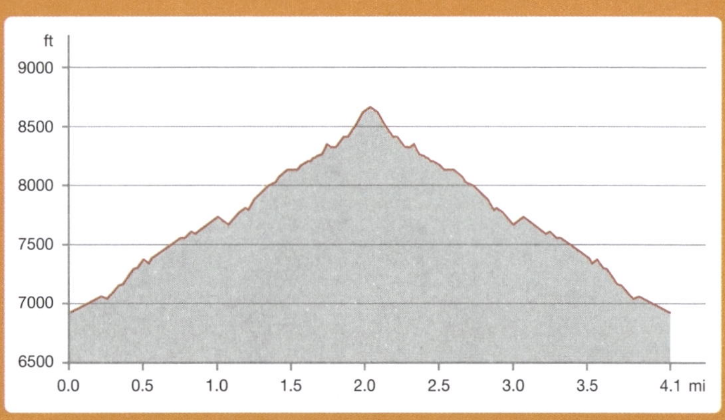

GRANITE LAKE AND MAGGIE'S PEAK

AN ALPINE LAKE AND LAKE TAHOE VIEWS

SOUTH LAKE TAHOE, CA

29

LENGTH

4.1 miles (round trip)

TIME & MONEY

2 hours 45 min., parking fee

ELEVATION GAIN

1,883 feet

DIFFICULTY

Strenuous

CONDITIONS

Year-round; partially shaded, snow gear required November–May

HIGHLIGHTS

Alpine lake, panoramic vistas

ESSENTIALS

- **Find the trailhead:** From the Heavenly Village in South Lake Tahoe, head west on Lake Tahoe Boulevard. In 4.7 miles, turn right onto CA-89 north/Emerald Bay Road. In 7.6 miles, the Inspiration Point parking lot is on your right, and the Bayview Day Use parking is on your left. Restrooms and trash bins are available at both Inspiration Point and Bayview parking lots. There are also a handful of free street parking spots on the side of Emerald Bay Road, across from the Inspiration Point lot.
- **Land manager:** U.S. Forest Service (fs.usda.gov)

WHY YOU'LL LOVE IT

- Lake Tahoe views from Maggie's Peak summit
- Alpine lake for your dog to swim in
- Sierra Nevada granite landscape

Climb to the pristine waters of Granite Lake for a chilly dip, and scramble up to Maggie's Peak summit.

This popular South Lake Tahoe hike is located in one of Lake Tahoe's busiest areas, but the views and alpine swimming opportunities are worth the crowds. Summer hikers should start early to secure parking, as the lots fill to capacity early in the day. In the winter, snow covers much of the trail, and only experienced winter hikers should attempt the hike.

From the Bayview Trailhead, you'll climb a series of switchbacks through a dense Jeffrey pine forest. Jeffrey pines dominate the lower elevations of Lake Tahoe because they can tolerate drastic temperature shifts, nutrient-poor granite soil, and other stressors like drought and fire. You can identify them by their bark's distinctive vanilla or butterscotch scent. You'll also find tall sugar pines mixed in with the Jeffrey pines. Sugar pine cones can reach up to 22 inches long—the largest cones of any pine species.

After climbing for half a mile, you'll take a quick 50-foot detour off the Bayview Trail to a vantage point of Lake Tahoe. From this viewpoint, you can see Emerald Bay and Fannette Island, Lake Tahoe's only island. Emerald Bay was carved by Ice Age glaciers, which gouged deep valleys into the granite bedrock. Geologists believe that Fannette Island survived the gouging because its granite was denser and more crystalline than the surrounding bedrock, making it harder for the glacial ice to carve it away.

Around a mile into the hike, you'll reach Granite Lake at 7,700 feet. This small but scenic alpine lake sits in a bowl that was also carved by glaciers during the Ice Age. Granite boulders and lodgepole pines line the lake's shores. Easy access points along the shoreline provide perfect spots where your dog (or you) can jump in for a refreshing swim.

This is a great place for a snack and water break before the more strenuous ascent to Maggie's Peak.

After Granite Lake, you'll gain 700 feet of elevation over a relentless three-quarter-mile stretch of switchbacks. As you climb higher, the terrain shifts to more granite boulders while the lower-elevation pines give way to red fir and mountain hemlock. When you reach the top of the switchbacks, you'll arrive at Maggie's Saddle, a prominent ridge connecting Maggie's North and South Peaks.

After the saddle, you'll turn off the Bayview Trail and scramble the remaining quarter mile to Maggie's South Peak. You'll get partial views of Lake Tahoe during your climb. From this point on, the trail remains unmarked, so keep a close eye on your route. There's quite a bit of scrambling over granite slabs and boulders, but it's doable for experienced dogs. You'll know you're at Maggie's Peak when you've reached the highest elevation possible. From the summit, you'll enjoy 360-degree views of Lake Tahoe's southern shore, the Crystal Range, and various alpine lakes within the Desolation Wilderness.

TURN-BY-TURN DIRECTIONS

1. The trailhead starts at the end of the Bayview Day Use lot. Take the Bayview Trail to the right of the trailhead kiosk, marked by a Desolation Wilderness signpost.
2. At 0.6 miles, take a short, 50-foot detour to your right for a view of Lake Tahoe. When you're ready, return to the trail and continue up the switchback.
3. At 1.1 miles, arrive at Granite Lake. Explore the lakeside to your left and continue on the Bayview Trail when you're ready.
4. At 1.8 miles, reach the saddle between Maggie's North and South Peaks. Turn left at the unmarked route to head to the south peak—you won't be going to the north peak. The trail disappears at this point, so scramble up the granite to reach the highest point.
5. At 2.0 miles, reach Maggie's South Peak. Enjoy the sweeping views of Lake Tahoe, and when you're ready, retrace your steps back to the trailhead.

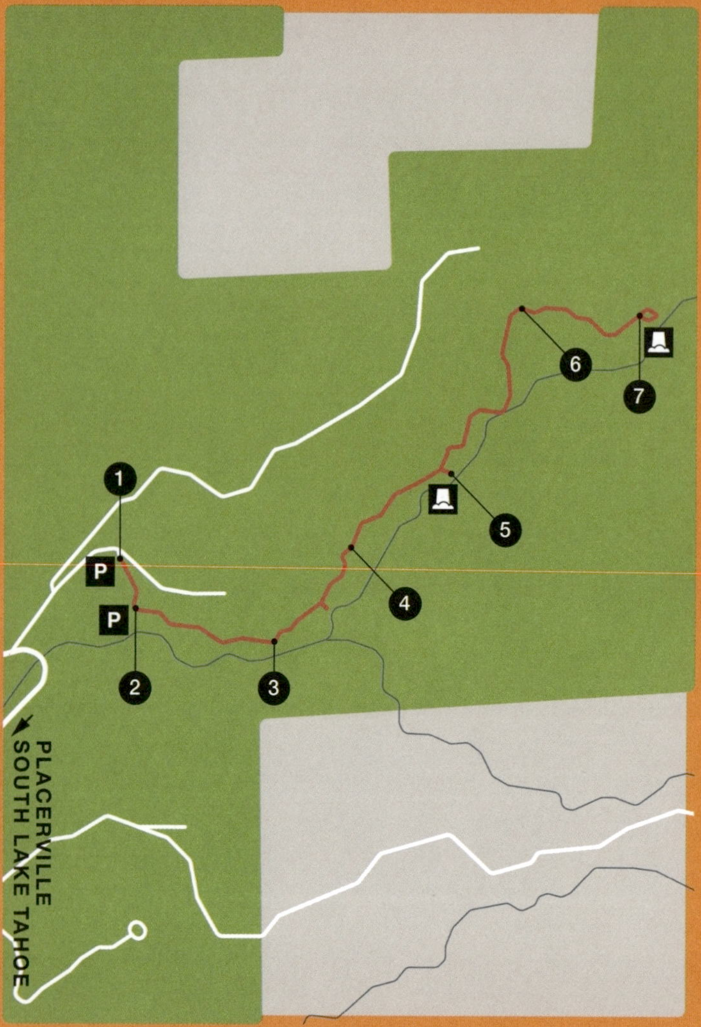

PLACERVILLE
SOUTH LAKE TAHOE

P Parking

Waterfall

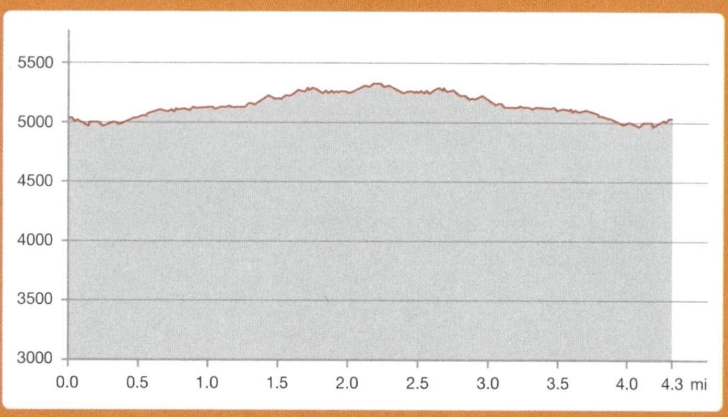

BASSI FALLS

A REWARDING HIKE TO CASCADING WATERFALLS

KYBURZ, CA

30

LENGTH
4.3 miles (round trip)

TIME & MONEY
2 hours, free

ELEVATION GAIN
355 feet

DIFFICULTY
Moderate

CONDITIONS
Year-round; mostly exposed, winter conditions from December–April

HIGHLIGHTS
Cascading waterfall, swimming holes

ESSENTIALS

- **Find the trailhead:** From the Heavenly Village in South Lake Tahoe, head west on Pioneer Trail Road. In 8.0 miles, turn left onto US-50 west. In 0.8 miles, go around the traffic circle and continue straight on US-50 west. In 30.4 miles, turn right onto Ice House Road. In 0.7 miles, turn right to stay on Ice House Road and proceed for 15.7 miles. At the intersection with Millionaire Camp Road, turn right and continue on the gravel road for 0.4 miles to reach the parking area. In the winter, roads to the trailhead may be difficult to access without 4WD. Check winter conditions before heading out. There are no facilities at the trailhead.
- **Land manager:** U.S. Forest Service (fs.usda.gov)

WHY YOU'LL LOVE IT

- Family-friendly hike will be accessible for many dogs
- Multiple swimming areas
- More rugged hiking area

Follow this mostly flat hike alongside a rushing creek to views of a cascading waterfall.

Bassi Falls sits at over 5,000 feet elevation in the rugged Crystal Basin area in El Dorado National Forest. The area was home to the Miwok, Maidu and Washoe peoples, who hunted and gathered in the lush landscape. The Washoe are the original inhabitants of Lake Tahoe and were traditionally divided into three regional groups in the north, east, and south. Despite speaking distinct variants of the Washoe language, the groups gathered for ceremonies and hunting drives. Cross-group marriages connected the communities across the region.

As you begin the hike, you'll immediately enter dense Jeffrey pine and incense cedar forest. Once you turn onto the Bassi Falls Trail, you'll hear Big Silver Creek flowing to your right. The trail follows Big Silver Creek and then Bassi Fork, a tributary of Big Silver Creek, upstream to the base of Bassi Falls. You'll hear the rushing water for most of your hike.

About half a mile into the hike, you'll reach your first view of Big Silver Creek. Swimming opportunities for you and your dog appear over the next quarter mile. Be mindful of water safety in the spring and early summer—high snowmelt will make the falls more dramatic but can make the creek dangerous for swimming. In summer, you may see western fence lizards basking on granite slabs along the creek. These native reptiles have distinctive blue bellies and throats. They also play an important ecological role—when ticks carrying Lyme disease feed on the lizards, their blood kills the Lyme bacteria.

As you follow the trail further upstream, you'll spot Lower Bassi Falls. This smaller cascade flows over granite slabs into inviting pools. You can swim in these pools while enjoying the view of the waterfall. As you approach the main Bassi Falls, you'll leave the forest and enter open, granite terrain. The last quarter mile offers many paths that go to the falls. The turn-by-turn directions follow one specific route, but feel free to explore different paths based on trail conditions or your own curiosity—you'll hear and see the falls ahead, so navigation is straightforward.

After traversing the granite landscape, you'll reach the spectacular Bassi Falls. Sierra Nevada snowmelt fuels the 100-foot waterfall. In a low snow season, the falls might be more of a trickle by late summer. The base of the falls is wide, and you can rock hop around to explore the area. Your dog can swim in the calmer pools about fifty feet downstream of the falls, as long as the water flow is safe. This is a remote hike with no facilities at the trailhead, so remember to bring enough water and pack out any dog waste.

TURN-BY-TURN DIRECTIONS

1. The trailhead starts at the signpost for "12N32F." Head straight onto the road.
2. At 0.2 miles, arrive at an alternate parking lot. This lot is not recommended for most hikers because the road is rough for low-clearance vehicles. Turn left at the signpost for the Bassi Creek Trail.
3. At 0.5 miles, the dirt trail has a brief section of rock slabs. Continue straight across the slabs for 300 feet before returning on the unmarked dirt trail.
4. At 0.9 miles, turn left at the unmarked junction. After 200 feet, continue straight at the signpost for Bassi Falls.
5. At 1.2 miles, arrive at Lower Bassi Falls.
6. At 1.8 miles, the forest opens up to rock slabs. Follow the unmarked trail on the right to cross the rock slabs and traverse toward the waterfalls.
7. At 2.1 miles, arrive at the base of Bassi Falls. Rock hop to get closer to the waterfalls. When you're done exploring the waterfalls, retrace your steps back to the parking lot.

1
2
3
4
5
6
7
8
9
10
11
12
13
14
P
SQUAW VALLEY

P Parking

ft
8000
7500
7000
6500
6000
0.0
0.5
1.0
1.5
2.0
2.5
3.0
3.5
3.8
mi

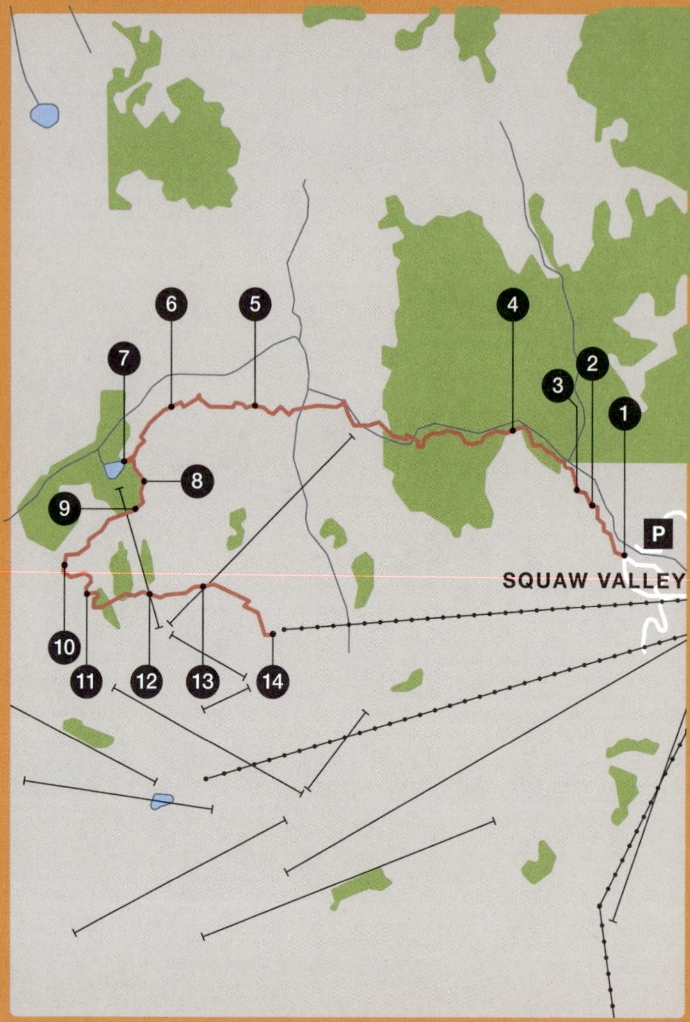

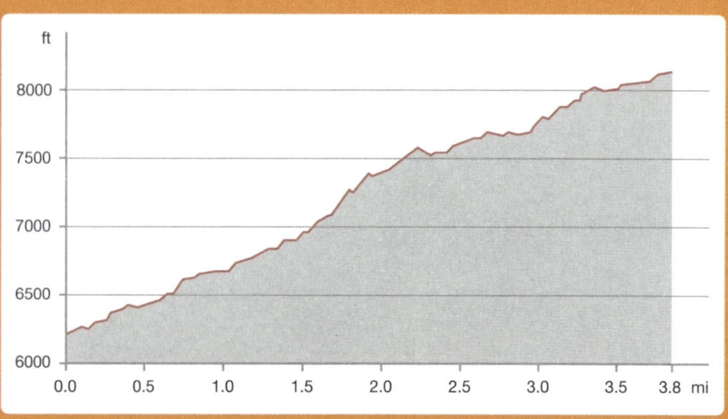

SHIRLEY LAKE AND HIGH CAMP

SCRAMBLE TO AN ALPINE LAKE AND TRAM

OLYMPIC VALLEY, CA

31

LENGTH

3.8 miles (point-to-point)

TIME & MONEY

2 hours 30 min. + 10 min. tram, free

ELEVATION GAIN

1,881 feet

DIFFICULTY

Strenuous

CONDITIONS

May–September exposed, rocky

HIGHLIGHTS

Granite boulders, aerial tram

ESSENTIALS

- 10-minute tram ride from High Camp down to the parking lot runs approximately every 20 minutes in the summer. See exact hours of operation on the Palisades Tahoe website. The tram down from High Camp is only dog-friendly in the summertime; dogs are not allowed during the winter ski season.
- **Find the trailhead:** From Truckee, take CA-89 South. In 7.8 miles, turn right onto Olympic Valley Road. In 2.3 miles, arrive at the parking lot for The Village at Palisades Tahoe. Park here. From the parking lot, walk on Olympic Valley Road toward the aerial tram. In 200 feet, turn right onto Shirley Canyon Road. Stay on Shirley Canyon Road until a dead end in 0.4 miles to reach the trailhead.
- **Land manager:** Palisades Tahoe (palisadestahoe.com)

WHY YOU'LL LOVE IT

- Lake for dogs to cool off in
- Tram ride with spectacular views
- Water for dogs available at High Camp

Scramble up granite boulders to an alpine lake and ride an aerial tram back down.

Palisades Tahoe, formerly known as Squaw Valley, famously hosted the 1960 Winter Olympics, marking the first time the Winter Olympic Games were hosted in the western United States. Today, Palisades Tahoe is arguably one of the best ski resorts in the United States. There are many areas in Palisades Tahoe that pay tribute to the Olympic Games, including the Olympic rings at the mountain entrance and the Olympic rings at the end of your hike.

This hike starts at Shirley Canyon Trailhead, off Shirley Canyon Road in the main Palisades Tahoe Village area. The approach into Shirley Canyon takes you on a steady climb through different pine trees, including Jeffrey pines and white firs. Along the hike, you may see yellow trail markers posted on trees or blue paint marked on rocks, guiding you to Shirley Lake. Along the ascent, you'll reach an area with large, granite slabs. There may be areas where you'll need to scramble and assist smaller or less agile dogs up the slabs. After scrambling up the slabs, you'll reach Shirley Lake. Shirley Lake is named after Shirley Scott, whose family members were some of the earliest white settlers in the Olympic Valley area.

After Shirley Lake, you'll continue on to High Camp. The trail to High Camp reminds you that you're hiking at a historic ski resort, because the trail takes you under the Solitude and Silverado Ski Lift Chairs and finishes at 8,200 feet. At High Camp, you'll be rewarded with expansive views of the Sierra Nevada and Lake Tahoe, additional Winter Olympics memorabilia, and a marketplace to stock up on drinks and snacks.

Your ride down from High Camp to the parking lot on the aerial tram takes you past the Tahoe Via Ferrata. Via Ferrata is Italian for "iron way" and consists of retrofitted steel ladder rungs and cables to help climbers get across previously inaccessible rock faces. Be sure to confirm the hours of operation for the aerial tram before you leave the trailhead to avoid the strenuous hike back down.

TURN-BY-TURN DIRECTIONS

1. From the Shirley Canyon Trailhead, head onto the signposted Shirley Canyon Trail.
2. At 0.2 miles, scramble up large rocks to stay on the Shirley Canyon Trail. You'll see the next yellow marking on a tree, straight ahead.
3. At 0.3 miles, reach another yellow marker and continue straight, to the right of the marker.
4. At 0.6 miles, cross a granite slab toward the yellow marker on a tree. Continue straight.
5. At 1.7 miles, cross a large area with granite slabs. Follow the blue paint markers on the slabs.
6. At 2.1 miles, keep following the blue paint markers on rocks to continue on the Shirley Canyon Trail.
7. At 2.4 miles, stay right at the blue "T" marker on a rock to Shirley Lake, 200 feet ahead. Once you've had your fill of Shirley Lake, head back to the blue "T" marker. Turn right to continue on Shirley Canyon Trail, away from Shirley Lake.
8. At 2.5 miles, follow the yellow marker on a tree to continue left on the Shirley Canyon Trail.
9. At 2.6 miles, continue straight, following the yellow marker on a tree.
10. At 2.9 miles, turn left and head up the unmarked gravel path uphill.
11. At 3.1 miles, there will be an unmarked trail on your left. Take this trail, which will climb up and away from the Shirley Lake Express Ski Lift.
12. At 3.4 miles, cross under the Solitude Ski Lift.
13. At 3.6 miles, cross under the Silverado Ski Lift.
14. At 3.8 miles, reach High Camp. When you're ready, take the aerial tram down.

TAHOE CITY
ALPINE MEADOWS
1
2
3
4
5
6
7
8
9
10
11
P
P Parking

ft
8000
7500
7000
6500
6000
0.0
0.5
1.0
1.5
2.0
2.5
3.0
3.5
4.0
4.5
4.8 mi

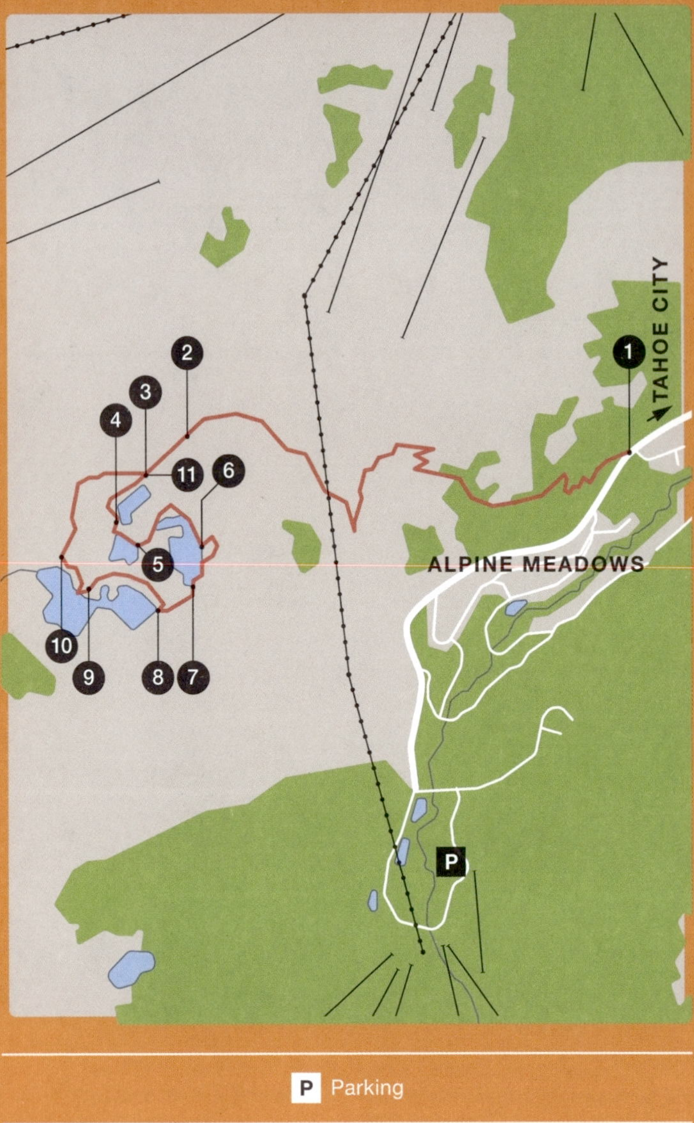

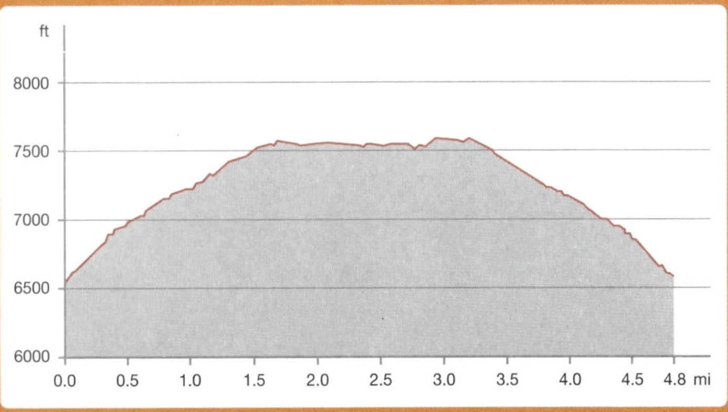

FIVE LAKES TRAIL

EXPLORE FIVE LAKES IN THE SIERRAS

ALPINE MEADOWS, CA

32

LENGTH
4.8 miles
(lollipop loop)

TIME & MONEY
3 hours,
free

ELEVATION GAIN
974 feet

DIFFICULTY
Moderate

CONDITIONS
May–November;
snowy in winter and
spring, mixed terrain

HIGHLIGHTS
Alpine scenery,
lake views

ESSENTIALS

- **Find the trailhead:** From Truckee, take CA-89 South. In 9.2 miles, turn right onto Alpine Meadows Road. In 2.1 miles, arrive at Five Lakes Trailhead at the intersection of Alpine Meadows Road and Deer Park Drive. Parking is available on the side of Alpine Meadows Road. The trail begins at the northwest side of Alpine Meadows Road.
- **Land manager:** Tahoe National Forest (fs.usda.gov/tahoe)

WHY YOU'LL LOVE IT

- Multiple lakes that dogs can swim in
- Beautiful spots to sit and have lunch
- Stable footing on trails to the lakes suitable for most dogs

Discover and swim in alpine lakes within the rugged Granite Chief Wilderness, with views of lush pine forests along the way.

Five Lakes Trail goes through the same area in the Granite Chief Wilderness as the famed Pacific Crest Trail. The Pacific Crest Trail is often considered one of the best thru-hiking trails in the U.S. because of its sheer diversity and length, spanning approximately 2,650 miles from the border with Mexico in California to the border with Canada in Washington. On this hike to Five Lakes Basin, you'll be able to see a similar landscape as those traversing the Pacific Crest Trail in this area.

The Granite Chief Wilderness was designated as a wilderness area in 1984 to preserve and protect the pristine nature. The Five Lakes Trail provides one of the most accessible ways to explore Granite Chief Wilderness.

Starting the hike, you'll take a dirt trail surrounded by Jeffrey pines into the Granite Chief Wilderness. Jeffrey pines are a prominent tree species in the Lake Tahoe region because they're well adapted to elevation and thrive in the drier soils. You may smell a slight scent of vanilla, pineapple, or butterscotch releasing from the Jeffrey pines' resin.

After the first mile, you'll pass under the Base to Base Gondola, which connects two different areas in the Palisades Tahoe ski resort. When you reach the Five Lakes Basin, you'll make a clockwise lollipop loop around the lakes, with an opportunity to stop at each.

The first lake is a great lake to swim in, with accessible entry points at both the north and south sides. The second, third, and fourth lakes are less accessible for swimming because the shorelines are less developed, with larger branches and other debris in the way. While the views are beautiful, the hike requires a bit of scrambling on rocks. If you prefer a more straightforward hike without the rocky trail, you can skip this section by heading straight after the first lake instead of turning left to the second lake (Step 4 in the turn-by-turn directions). This will lead directly to the fifth lake.

The fifth is the best lake to swim in because it's the biggest lake and has cleaner, deeper water for your dogs. The path along the lake is also more developed, so there are different areas along the shoreline where you can dip in for a swim. Walking around the lake, you'll find areas where you can stop to eat lunch or lay out a hammock between the trees.

TURN-BY-TURN DIRECTIONS

1. From the trailhead sign, head left onto the Five Lakes Trail.
2. At 1.6 miles, pass a sign for Tahoe National Forest. You're now in Granite Chief Wilderness. Continue straight on the Five Lakes Trail.
3. At 1.7 miles, reach a fork in the road marked with a "No camping or stock within 300 ft of water" sign; turn left at this sign. After 300 feet, reach the first lake. Continue straight to wrap around the lake. The trail is defined but unmarked.
4. At 1.9 miles, reach another optional resting point for the first lake on your left. When you're ready, continue straight to head to the second lake. After 150 feet, take a left at an unmarked fork in the trail to arrive at the second lake.
5. At 2.0 miles, the trail leaves the second lake and becomes rocky. Continue straight on the unmarked trail.
6. At 2.2 miles, reach the third lake. When you're ready, continue straight on the unmarked trail heading around the shoreline of the third lake.
7. At 2.4 miles, leave the third lake and head toward the fourth lake on the same unmarked trail.
8. At 2.5 miles, reach the fourth lake. Continue straight on the unmarked trail to trace the northern edge of the lake.
9. At 2.7 miles, reach an unmarked fork in the road and turn left. After 200 feet, reach the fifth lake. When you're ready, continue straight. Over the next 0.2 miles, there are multiple entry points into the fifth lake for your dogs, but we will head back to the first lake after 0.1 miles.
10. At 2.8 miles, take the defined but unmarked trail away from the fifth lake, back toward the first lake.
11. At 3.1 miles, reach the fork with the "no camping or stock" sign. To head back to the parking lot, stay left, retracing your steps on the Five Lakes Trail back to the trailhead.

GREATER SACRAMENTO

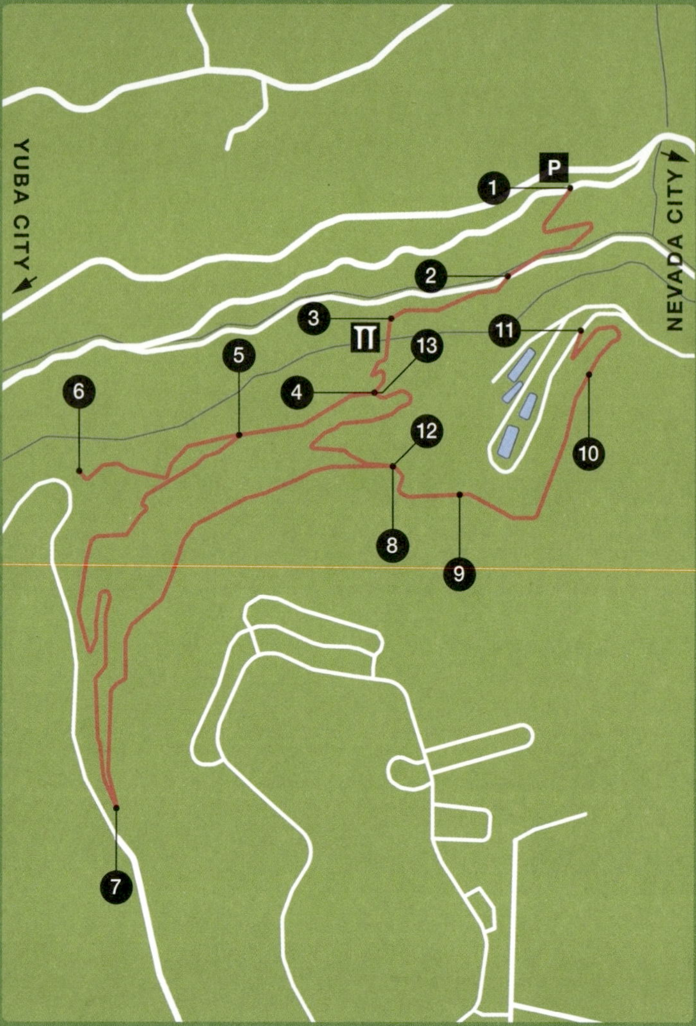

YUBA CITY

NEVADA CITY

P Parking

Bridge

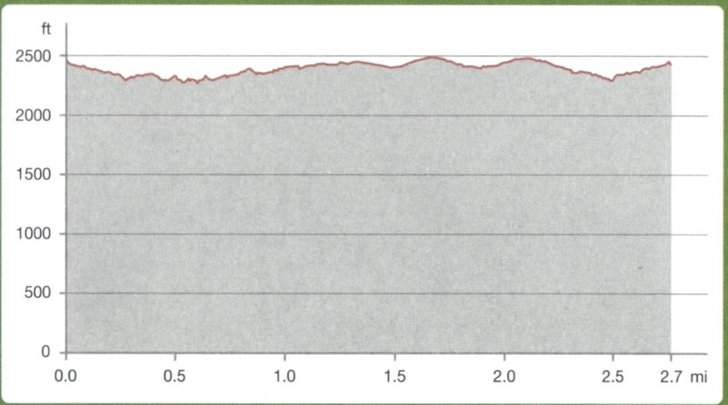

DEER CREEK TRIBUTE TRAIL

MEANDER THROUGH A HISTORIC MINING TOWN

NEVADA CITY, CA

33

LENGTH
2.7 miles (round trip)

TIME & MONEY
2 hours, free

ELEVATION GAIN
653 feet

DIFFICULTY
Moderate

CONDITIONS
Year-round; mostly shaded

HIGHLIGHTS
Suspension bridge, historic site

ESSENTIALS

- **Find the trailhead:** From downtown Sacramento, head onto CA-160 north. In 2.4 miles, merge onto Interstate 80 Business Loop east. In 4.4 miles, merge onto Interstate 80 east toward Reno. In 24.4 miles, take the exit for CA-49 toward Grass Valley/Placerville. In 0.2 miles, turn left onto CA-49 north/Grass Valley Highway. In 27.2 miles, take the exit for Broad Street. In 0.2 miles, turn left onto Broad Street and proceed for 0.3 miles, passing through Nevada City's historic downtown district. Turn left onto Bennett Street. In 0.1 miles, turn left onto Monroe Street. In 0.2 miles, continue onto Old Downieville Highway. In 0.3 miles, take a slight left onto Champion Mine Road. 350 feet ahead, you'll find limited parking on the right side of the street.

- **Land manager:** Maintained for the City of Nevada City by Bear Yuba Land Trust (bylt.org)

WHY YOU'LL LOVE IT

- Beautiful creek views from a suspension bridge
- Interpretive displays on native peoples
- Nearby historic downtown with dog-friendly amenities

Cross a dramatic suspension bridge and meander through lush woodlands. Along the way, stop to read various interpretive signs about the Nisenan people and the area's mining heritage.

Nevada City was established in the 1850s, when prospectors rushed to the banks of Deer Creek in search of gold. Long before the Gold Rush, the Nisenan people called this land Oustomah. At one point, the Nisenan had a population of 2,000, but they suffered devastating losses during the Gold Rush period—many Nisenan perished from foreign diseases or were killed as gold seekers poured in. The frenzy reshaped their ancestral lands, replacing forests and hillsides with mining districts carved by axes and dynamite. The Deer Creek Tribute Trail honors the area's rich and complex history.

Within the first quarter mile, you'll cross a 150-foot-long suspension bridge named Angkula Seo, the traditional name for Deer Creek. Below, you'll hear Deer Creek roaring as it flows from the Sierra Nevada foothills. Deer Creek is home to important salmon and steelhead populations, and its flow can be especially strong in the months following heavy rain and snowfall.

Shortly after you cross the bridge, you'll take a detour to the remnants of the Providence Mine—one of the largest-producing gold mines in Nevada City, producing over $8 million in gold and silver. Gold mining involved digging angled shafts to access "veins," which are ribbon-like formations of gold-containing rock. Miners create interconnected tunnels as they discover "ore shoots," which are sections in the veins with the most gold. Providence Mine had a main shaft that went down 1,250 feet and had ten horizontal levels extending about 2,000 feet, following the gold veins.

The woodlands along the trail support a variety of plant species, including ponderosa pine and live oak, and provide habitat for California quail, which display distinctive comma-shaped head plumes. These ground-dwelling birds feast on native lupine seeds, beetles, ants, and seasonal acorns and berries that abound in the Sierra foothills.

As you reach the end of the trail, you can take a closer look at more plant species in the labyrinth-shaped Nisenan Garden. The garden highlights plants such as purple-flowered violets and strap-leafed soaproot that held important medicinal and practical uses for the Nisenan peoples for generations. Soaproot, for example, can be boiled and used as glue, crushed for fishing, or mixed with water to create soap.

TURN-BY-TURN DIRECTIONS

1. From the trailhead, head onto the signposted Deer Creek Tribute Trail.
2. At 0.1 miles, continue straight at the marked junction to continue on the Deer Creek Tribute Trail.
3. At 0.2 miles, turn left onto the suspension bridge. After crossing the bridge, turn right. After 100 feet, reach an unmarked junction. The trail to your right leads to a bench; ignore this and take the left trail.
4. At 0.3 miles, turn right at the junction onto the marked Nisenan Loop Trail. The Nisenan Loop Trail is part of the Deer Creek Tribute Trail system, so you'll see signage for both trails along the route.
5. At 0.4 miles, turn right at the marked junction for the Providence Mine Spur Trail.
6. In 0.6 miles, reach the Providence Mine. When you're ready, head back to the junction from Step 5 and continue on the Nisenan Loop Trail.
7. At 1.1 miles, turn left at the marked junction to continue on the Deer Creek Tribute Trail.
8. At 1.5 miles, continue straight at the marked junction to stay on the Deer Creek Tribute Trail.
9. At 1.6 miles, turn left at the marked junction to take a short detour to the Nisenan Garden. When you're ready, continue on the Deer Creek Tribute Trail.
10. At 1.7 miles, keep left at the sign to continue on the Deer Creek Tribute Trail.
11. At 1.9 miles, reach the end of the trail. Poop bags are often available at this trailhead. Turn around and return the way you came, back to Step 8.
12. At 2.2 miles, reach the junction from Step 8 and take the right trail marked as "Lower Trail."
13. At 2.4 miles, reach the junction from Step 4; turn right and retrace your steps to return to the parking area.

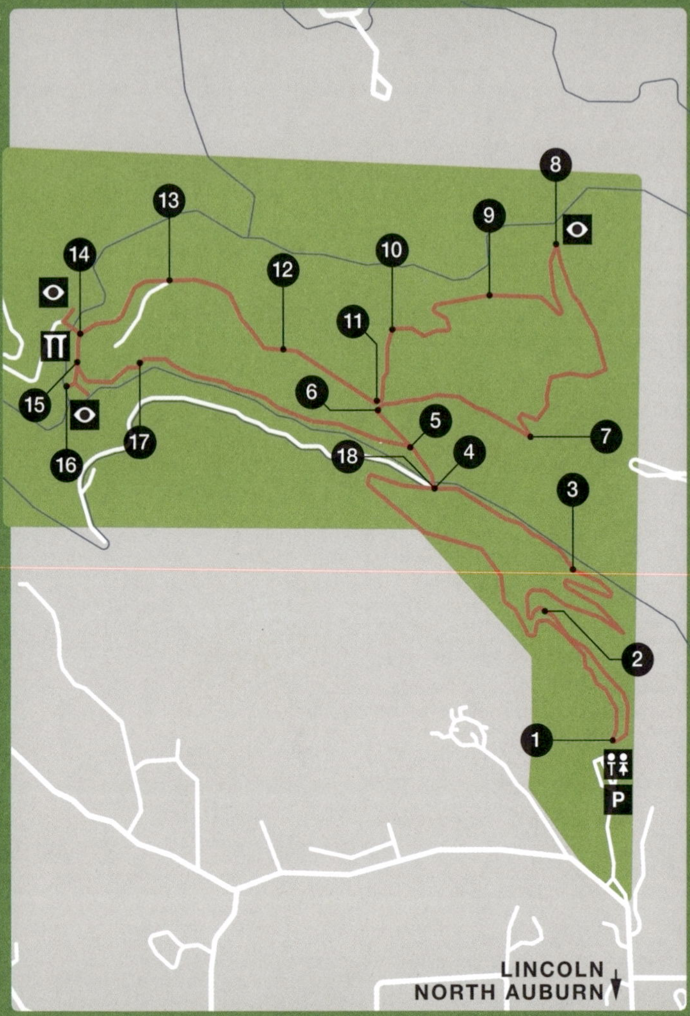

LINCOLN
NORTH AUBURN

P Parking | Toilet | Viewpoint | Bridge

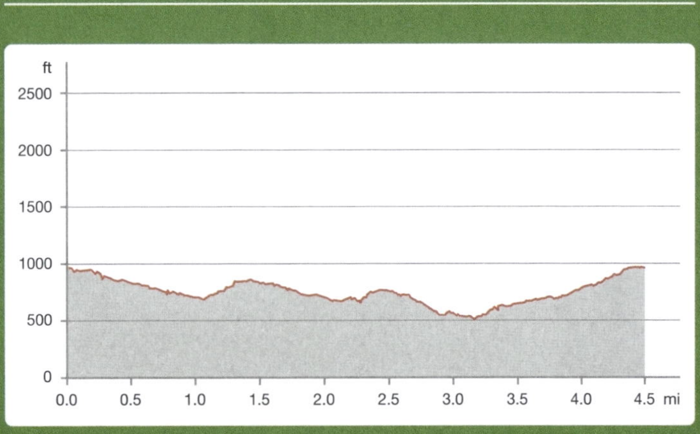

SEVEN POOLS AND HIDDEN FALLS

WATERFALL VIEWS AND A SWIMMING HOLE

AUBURN, CA

34

LENGTH
4.5 miles (loop)

TIME & MONEY
2 hours 30 min., parking fee

ELEVATION GAIN
617 feet

DIFFICULTY
Moderate

CONDITIONS
Year-round; partially exposed

HIGHLIGHTS
Scenic views, waterfall

ESSENTIALS

- **Find the trailhead:** From downtown Sacramento, head north on 16th Street. In 1.3 miles, continue onto CA-160 north. In 2.4 miles, merge onto I-80 Business Loop east. In 4.4 miles, merge onto I-80 east toward Reno and proceed for 21.4 miles. Take the exit for CA-193 west toward Lincoln. In 0.1 miles, merge onto CA-193 west. In 0.2 miles, take a slight right onto Ophir Road and continue for 0.3 miles. Turn left onto Lozanos Road. In 1.0 miles, turn right onto Bald Hill Road and proceed for 2.5 miles. At Mt. Vernon Road, turn left and continue for 3.7 miles. Turn right onto Mears Drive. In 0.5 miles, turn right onto Mears Place. After 0.2 miles, turn right to enter Hidden Falls Regional Park. The parking lot is 0.2 miles ahead with restrooms, water fountains, picnic tables, and trash bins. An advanced parking reservation may be required on weekends, holidays, and other high-usage days.
- **Land manager:** Placer County (placer.ca.gov)

WHY YOU'LL LOVE IT

- Well-maintained trails are accessible for most dogs
- Multiple vistas of canyons and waterfalls
- Calm swimming hole

Hike to views of granite pools and swim in calm creek waters below Hidden Falls on one of Placer County's most popular family-friendly hikes.

Hidden Falls Regional Park sits in the oak woodlands of the Sierra Nevada foothills near Auburn, a historic Gold Rush town. Auburn served as a major supply hub during the California Gold Rush and later became a key railroad town with the arrival of the transcontinental railroad in the 1860s. Now, many travelers pass through Auburn en route to Lake Tahoe, but this area offers some of Northern California's most rewarding hiking destinations.

You'll start your hike on the Poppy Trail, a dirt path that descends gently through oak woodland. In the spring, you'll see various wildflowers including blue dicks, white globe lily, and harvest brodiaea. In the cooler months, you'll see green-leafed miner's lettuce. Gold Rush miners ate this vitamin C–rich plant to prevent scurvy, a nutritional deficiency widespread during the 1850s. However, Native Americans had been consuming miner's lettuce for centuries before miners ever arrived in California.

Around a mile in, you'll turn onto the Blue Oak Loop Trail, which leads deeper into the oak woodlands. This quiet dirt trail winds through shaded forest with occasional signs about local birds and wildlife. After about a mile on the Blue Oak Loop Trail, you'll see the Seven Pools at the base of a steep drop-off straight ahead. Be careful not to let your dog pull you off the rocky vista. Small cascades separate each pool, creating a stunning natural staircase of water along Raccoon Creek.

After Seven Pools, you'll make your way to the North Legacy Way fire road. You'll be on North Legacy Way for about half a mile as you pass wildflowers like bowltube iris. Around three miles from the trailhead, you'll cross the Canyon View Bridge and head up a few rocky steps onto the Canyon View observation deck. From the deck, you'll have expansive views of Canyon View Bridge, Raccoon Creek, and Canyon View Falls.

After the observation deck, you'll make your final approach to the platform overlooking the 30-foot Hidden Falls. The falls flow year-round but are most spectacular in winter and spring when fed by rainfall. From the observation deck, you can follow a short scramble down to the base of the falls along Raccoon Creek. This popular swimming spot offers calm pools perfect for dogs to cool off. There are often families gathering here, so be sure to keep dogs on leash and under control when others are present.

You'll return to the parking lot via South Legacy Way, a wide fire road. The return journey is a gradual climb through shaded woodland bordered by spring wildflowers. You'll hike the final quarter mile in full sun as you approach the parking lot.

TURN-BY-TURN DIRECTIONS

1. From the parking lot, walk through the gate. In 50 feet, take the Poppy Trail on the right, toward the sign for "Waterfalls."
2. At 0.3 miles, go straight at the unmarked junction. In 25 feet, keep left at the unmarked fork to continue on the Poppy Trail.
3. At 0.8 miles, continue straight at the unmarked junction, ignoring a trail on the right, which goes to Deadman Creek. This entry point into Deadman Creek can be dangerous, especially during high water flow.
4. At 1.0 miles, reach a multi-trail junction with a trail map and trash bin; turn right at the signpost onto North Legacy Way.
5. At 1.1 miles, turn right onto the signposted Blue Oak Loop Trail.
6. At 1.2 miles, reach another multi-trail junction with a trail map; turn right at the signpost to continue on the Blue Oak Loop Trail.
7. At 1.4 miles, turn left onto the signposted Seven Pools Vista Trail.
8. At 1.8 miles, reach Seven Pools Vista. When you're ready, take the unmarked trail on the right.
9. At 2.0 miles, turn left onto the signposted Seven Pools Loop.
10. At 2.3 miles, turn left onto the signposted Pond Turtle Trail.
11. At 2.4 miles, reach the junction from Step 6; turn right onto the gravel North Legacy Way to continue to the waterfalls.
12. At 2.5 miles, continue straight at the signposted junction to stay on North Legacy Way.
13. At 2.7 miles, keep right at the signposted fork to stay on North Legacy Way.
14. At 2.9 miles, cross the bridge at the signposted junction. At the end of the bridge, turn right to the Canyon View observation deck. When you're ready, return to the beginning of the bridge and turn right at the signpost for the Hidden Falls Overlook.
15. At 3.0 miles, turn right at the unmarked fork down to the waterfalls. There'll be small trails on your right to Raccoon Creek, but continue straight to the Hidden Falls overlook platform, 260 feet ahead. After viewing the falls, return back to the small trails and head down to Raccoon Creek.
16. At 3.1 miles, reach Racoon Creek. When you're ready, return to Step 15 and turn right onto the Hidden Falls Access Trail, away from Raccoon Creek.
17. At 3.3 miles, pass a trash bin and turn right at the junction with a sign for Hidden Falls Overlook.
18. At 3.8 miles, return to Step 4. Ignore the Poppy Trail on your left and the westbound direction of South Legacy Way on your right. Take the middle trail, which is the southbound direction of South Legacy Way. Continue on South Legacy Way back to the parking lot, ignoring any side trails.

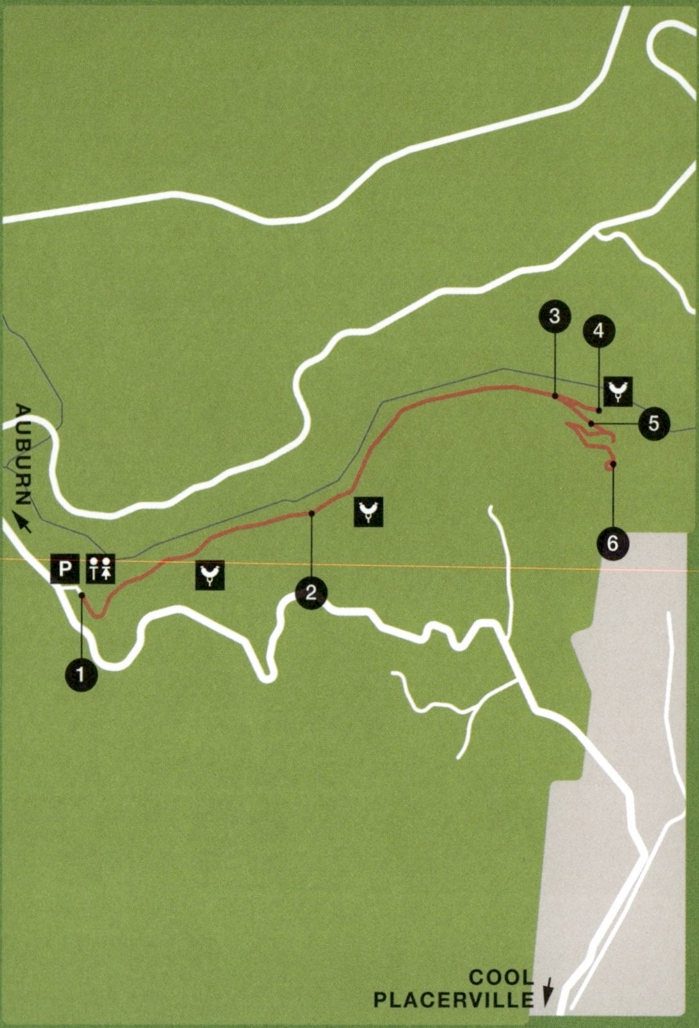

AUBURN

COOL
PLACERVILLE

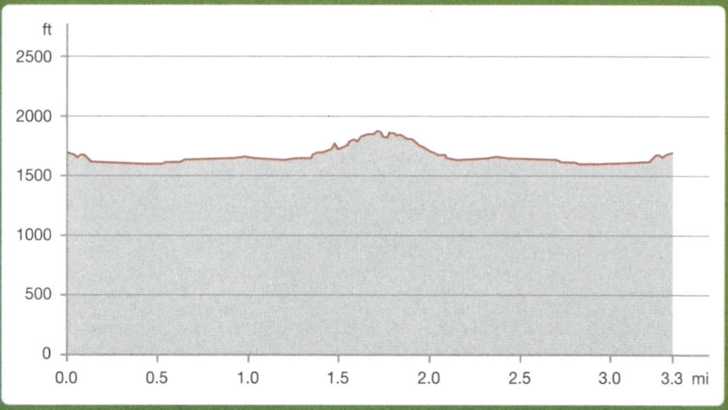

QUARRY TRAIL

A HISTORIC TRAIL TO A LIMESTONE QUARRY

AUBURN, CA

35

LENGTH
3.3 miles
(round trip)

TIME & MONEY
1 hour 30 min.,
parking fee

ELEVATION GAIN
252 feet

DIFFICULTY
Easy

CONDITIONS
Year-round;
mostly exposed

HIGHLIGHTS
Scenic river
views, historic
cave

ESSENTIALS

- **Find the trailhead:** From downtown Auburn, head northeast on Lincoln Way toward Harrison Avenue. In 0.2 miles, turn right onto CA-49 south and continue for 2.3 miles. Turn right onto CA-193 east/CA-49 south. In 0.4 miles, turn left onto Quarry Trail Road. The parking lot is 300 feet ahead.
- **Land manager:** California State Parks (parks.ca.gov)

WHY YOU'LL LOVE IT

- Wide, flat trail will be accessible for most dogs
- Historic limestone cave
- Watch people rock climbing in the quarry

Hike along the Middle Fork American River to Hawver Cave and a spectacular limestone quarry. This wide trail offers glimpses into California's limestone-mining history.

Auburn State Recreation Area sits in the heart of California's Gold Country, where the North and Middle Forks of the American River converge. These two rivers carved steep canyons, and their gold-laden banks drew thousands of gold miners in the mid-1800s. After the Gold Rush era, the Mountain Quarries Railroad used this trail to transport limestone from the quarry to Auburn.

The first mile of the Quarry Trail takes you on a wide path above the Middle Fork of the American River. The Middle Fork was one of the richest mining areas in California during the Gold Rush. A 1890 report estimated an average take of $1 million of placer gold per mile. On this trail, you'll walk through foothill woodland, an ecosystem of oak trees, shrubs, and grassland typical of California's lower elevations, which was shaped by both the river and the hydraulic blasting of the Gold Rush. In spring and early summer, you'll see wildflowers such as cardinal catchflies and blue dicks, plus purple flowers blooming on the western redbud trees.

Roughly a mile and a quarter in, you'll reach the Cave Valley limestone area. During its operation, the Mountain Quarries Mine was the largest limestone quarry in Northern California. Limestone served various industrial applications, including cement and steel production. You'll see historic remnants of the limestone-processing structures towering high above, along with informational signage detailing the quarry's history.

Next, you'll climb a couple of hundred feet to view the processing structures from behind and arrive at the tunnel entrance to Hawver Cave. In 1906, a group of students discovered bones of prehistoric mammals such as saber-toothed cats and ground sloths in the cave. Archaeologists also discovered human skeletal remains dating back 10,000 years. Paleontologists investigated the cave for several years before the Mountain Quarries Company converted it to a limestone mine. During its peak, close to 200 men mined 1,000 to 1,500 tons of limestone per day. The tunnel to Hawver Cave is currently closed to the public, but you can read informational signs posted outside the gate.

After leaving Hawver Cave, you'll have a final climb to the Auburn Quarry climbing area, also known as Cave Valley. The California Department of Parks and Recreation opened the area to recreational rock climbing in 2012 after lobbying efforts from the Climbing Resource Advocates for Greater Sacramento and Access Fund. While you and your dog watch from the trail, you may see climbers on marked sections of the limestone walls.

TURN-BY-TURN DIRECTIONS

1. The trailhead begins past the gate, where there are restrooms, a trash bin, and dog waste bags available. Continue straight to start on the Quarry Trail.
2. At 0.6 miles, continue straight on the Quarry Trail, ignoring an unmarked trail on your right.
3. At 1.2 miles, stay left at the unmarked fork.
4. At 1.3 miles, reach the Cave Valley limestone area with picnic tables and trash bins. When you're ready, return the way you came, back to the fork from Step 3, and turn left at the fork toward the marked Hawver Cave.
5. At 1.4 miles, continue straight, ignoring the unmarked trail on your left. After 200 feet, continue straight at the junction, ignoring the sign for "climbing area" on your right. After another 220 feet, reach Hawver Cave Gate A. When you're ready, return to the "climbing area" sign and turn left.
6. At 1.7 miles, reach the climbing area with multiple rock walls. When you're ready, retrace your steps to return to the parking lot, ignoring your previous detours for Hawver Cave Gate A and Cave Valley limestone area.

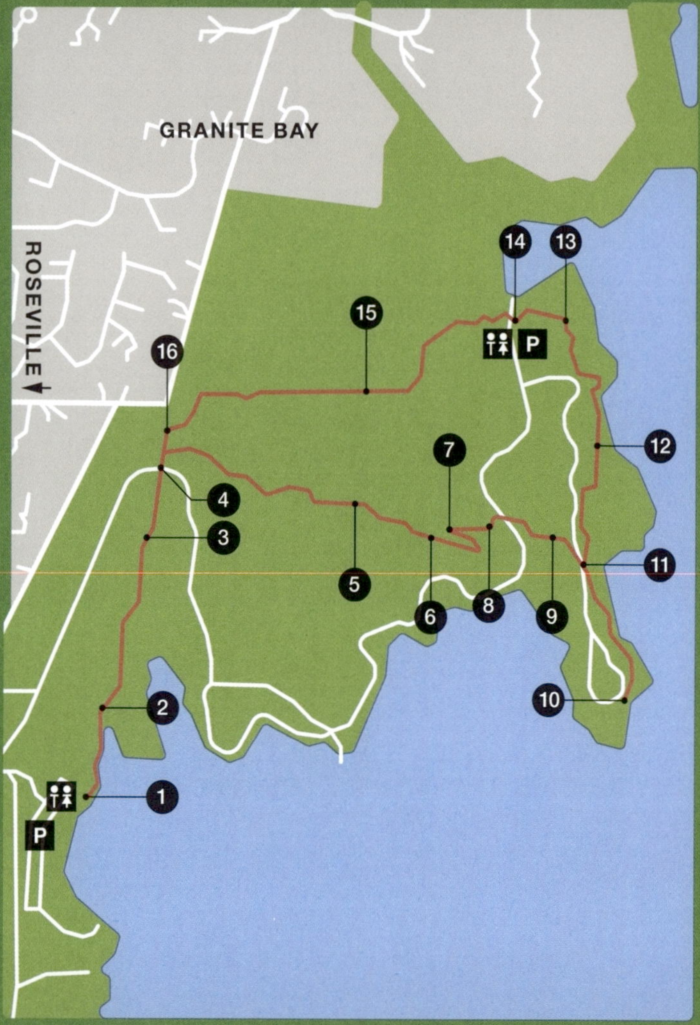

GRANITE BAY
ROSEVILLE
1
2
3
4
5
6
7
8
9
10
11
12
13
14
15
16
P
P

P Parking

Toilet

ft
2500
2000
1500
1000
500
0
0.0
0.5
1.0
1.5
2.0
2.5
3.0
3.5
4.0
4.3 mi

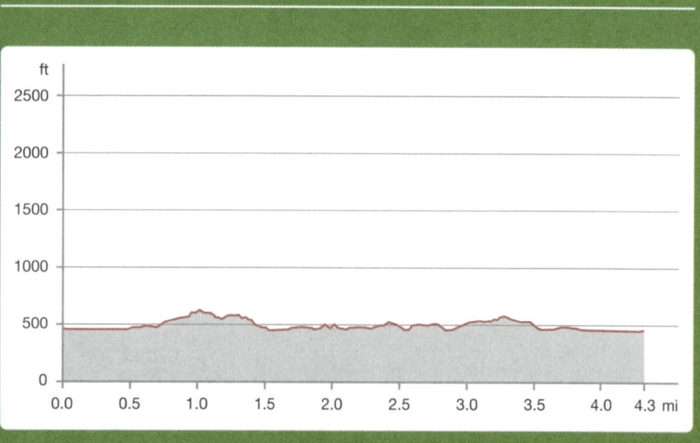

FOLSOM LAKE

A STUNNING LAKESIDE HIKE WITH SWIMMING

GRANITE BAY, CA

36

LENGTH

4.3 miles
(lollipop loop)

TIME & MONEY

2 hours,
parking fee

ELEVATION GAIN

379 feet

DIFFICULTY

Moderate

CONDITIONS

Year-round; mostly exposed, may require navigation if trails are submerged

HIGHLIGHTS

Lake swimming, scenic overlooks

ESSENTIALS

- **Find the trailhead:** From downtown Sacramento, head east on N Street toward 11th Street. In 0.5 miles, turn left onto 16th Street. In 1.6 miles, continue onto CA-160 north. In 2.4 miles, merge onto I-80 Business Loop east and proceed for 4.4 miles until you merge onto I-80 East toward Reno. In 8.8 miles, take the exit for Douglas Boulevard east and merge onto Douglas Boulevard. After 6.4 miles, Douglas Boulevard turns slightly right and becomes Park Road at the Folsom Lake entrance kiosk. In 0.9 miles, turn right into the Granite Bay parking lot, where there are picnic tables, restrooms, and water fountains.
- **Land manager:** California State Parks (parks.ca.gov)

WHY YOU'LL LOVE IT

- Multiple lake access points for dogs
- Varied terrain to scenic overlooks
- Potential spring wildflower superbloom

Explore multiple trails around Folsom Lake, including the swimming spots at Granite Bay, scenic overlooks at Dotons Point, and spring wildflowers at Beeks Bight.

Completed in 1956, Folsom Dam created this 11,500-acre reservoir for flood control and water supply. The lake sits where the American River once flowed freely through granite canyons. Folsom Lake still provides water to the surrounding area, but it has also become a popular destination for recreational activities such as fishing, boating, and hiking.

Your adventure begins at Granite Bay, where the developed beach area offers restrooms, picnic tables, and a snack bar. While dogs aren't allowed on the main beach, they can swim at any of the access points along the natural shoreline a couple hundred yards north. Leaving the shoreline, you'll head inland on an exposed connector trail.

The next part of your journey moves away from the shoreline and into oak woodland on the Center Trail. Interior live oaks and blue oaks provide shade during the warmer months, helping keep your dog cool. In the spring and early summer, you'll encounter colorful wildflowers such as orange bush monkey flower, California poppy, and narrowleaf mule's ears—native plants that resemble mini sunflowers. You'll also pass a popular tree swing that overlooks the lake.

The trail descends south to Dotons Point, passing benches where you can pause to enjoy the scenery and search for pipevine swallowtail butterflies. These black-and-blue butterflies are often seen in spring, summer, and sometimes early fall. Pipevine swallowtail caterpillars have adapted to eat California pipevine, a plant that is toxic to most other animals. From Dotons Point, you'll have panoramic vistas of Folsom Lake and the surrounding Sierra Nevada foothills. You can also look across the lake to Granite Bay, where you started, just two miles back. If you make a quick detour down to the shoreline, your dog can swim in the calm water.

As you continue north from Dotons Point, you'll head toward Beeks Bight, a wildflower superbloom hotspot. However, blooms aren't guaranteed every year. The wildflowers require lots of winter rain, but not enough that the lake rises too high and covers the lupine flower fields. If you're fortunate enough to visit during a bloom, please stay with your dog on designated trails to avoid trampling flowers.

For your return journey, you'll take the Pioneer Express Trail back to Granite Bay. This trail traces part of the historic path Gold Rush pioneers took to reach mining camps along the American River. Though the miners are long gone, horseback riders and hikers still use the trail. Your last half mile leads back to the Shoreline Trail. This is a final chance for your dog to cool off in the water before you return to Granite Bay.

TURN-BY-TURN DIRECTIONS

1. The unmarked, sandy trail begins at the corner of Granite Bay Main Beach, to the left of lifeguard tower 1. Follow the trail along the lake shoreline for 400 feet. Your dog can enter the water here at any point once you leave Granite Bay Main Beach.
2. At 0.1 miles, continue straight on the unmarked, sandy trail. When the lake is high, this trail may be underwater. If that's the case, take the trail on your left running parallel. Both of these trails lead to the same point.
3. At 0.5 miles, continue straight on the unmarked, sandy trail.
4. At 0.6 miles, cross the paved Park Road. In 50 feet, continue straight at an unmarked junction. After 100 feet, take a left at the unmarked junction and take the first right onto the signposted Center Trail.
5. At 1.0 miles, continue straight on the Center Trail at the unmarked junction.
6. At 1.2 miles, continue straight on the Center Trail at the unmarked junction.
7. At 1.4 miles, turn right at the unmarked junction to continue on the Center Trail.
8. At 1.5 miles, turn right at the unmarked junction and cross the paved Park Road. In 25 feet, turn right at the signposted "Granite Bay Multi-Use Trail." If this turn is submerged, take a left instead and follow the trail for 0.3 miles, continuously turning right when possible.
9. At 1.6 miles, turn left onto the unmarked trail. After 100 feet, both trail options from Step 8 arrive at this junction, where there are picnic tables and trash bins. Cross the paved Park Road and turn right onto the unmarked Dotons Point Trail.
10. At 2.0 miles, reach Dotons Point. When you're done exploring, retrace your steps back to the Dotons Point Trail, and walk north on the Dotons Point Trail.
11. At 2.3 miles, continue straight, ignoring the unmarked path on the left.
12. At 2.5 miles, continue straight on the Dotons Point Trail.
13. At 2.8 miles, turn left at the unmarked fork.
14. At 2.9 miles, arrive at Beeks Bight. When you're ready, cross the parking lot and then head onto an unmarked dirt trail, passing restrooms. 50 feet after passing the restrooms, take a slight right at the unmarked fork to reach the signpost that says "horseback riding and hiking trail only." Turn left at the signpost to follow the Pioneer Express Trail.
15. At 3.2 miles, the trail splits into short sections of unmarked trails that all converge back onto the Pioneer Express Trail. Continue straight over the next 0.2 miles at these junctions.
16. At 3.6 miles, take the unmarked fork on your left. In 200 feet, reach the junction from Step 4. Retrace your steps back to the parking lot.

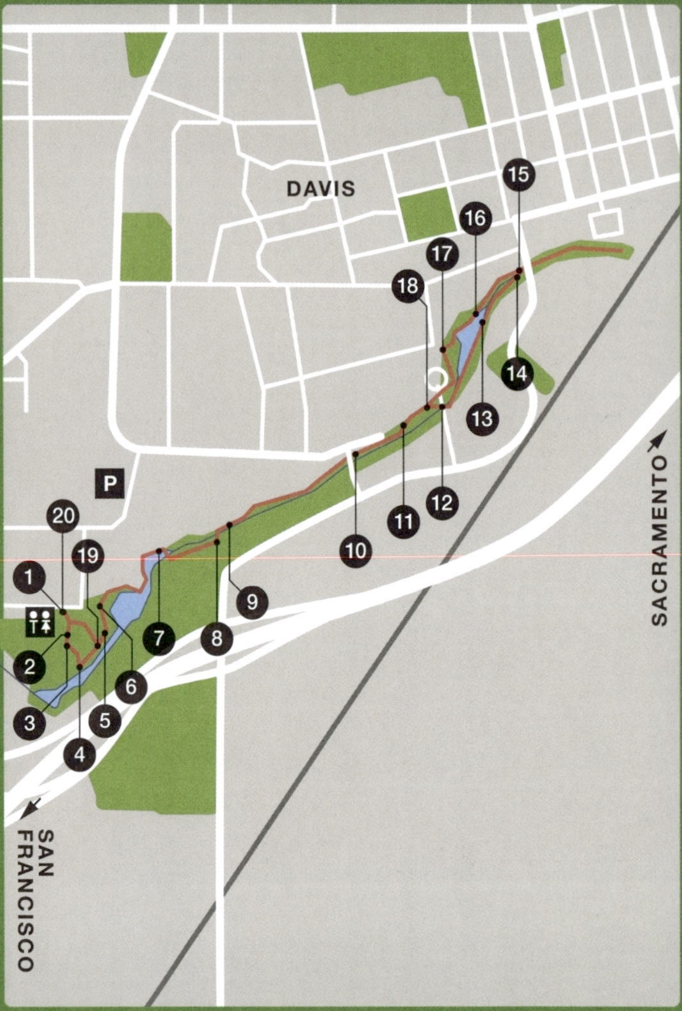

DAVIS
P
20
19
1
2
3
4
5
6
7
8
9
10
11
12
13
14
15
16
17
18
SACRAMENTO
SAN FRANCISCO

P Parking

Toilet

ft
2500
2000
1500
1000
500
0
0.0
0.5
1.0
1.5
2.0
2.5
3.0
3.5
3.7 mi

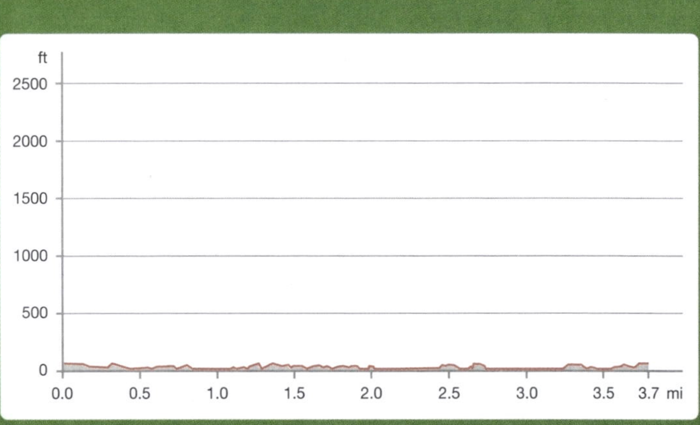

UC DAVIS ARBORETUM

AN EDUCATIONAL AND ECOLOGICAL HIKE

DAVIS, CA

37

LENGTH
3.7 miles
(loop)

TIME & MONEY
1 hour 45 min.,
weekends/
holidays free

ELEVATION GAIN
62 feet

DIFFICULTY
Easy

CONDITIONS
Year-round;
mostly paved,
partially exposed

HIGHLIGHTS
Diverse plants,
outdoor museum

ESSENTIALS

- **Find the trailhead:** From Sacramento, take Interstate 80 West. In 10.6 miles, take the exit for UC Davis. In 0.3 miles, turn right onto Old Davis Road and proceed for 0.4 miles. At the traffic circle, take the second exit onto La Rue Road. In 0.1 miles, turn left to stay on La Rue Road. In 0.4 miles, turn left onto Garrod Drive. In 0.2 miles, turn left to stay on Garrod Drive. The trailhead starts 0.2 miles ahead on Garrod Drive. Street parking is available on Garrod Drive or at Visitor Parking Lot 55 on Garrod Drive. Parking is free on weekends and holidays. For weekdays and special events, parking must be paid for on the Pay-to-Park App AggiePark.
- **Land manager:** UC Davis Arboretum and Public Garden (arboretum.ucdavis.edu)

WHY YOU'LL LOVE IT

- Demonstration gardens and interpretive signs highlight a wide variety of both California native and non-local plant species
- Exploring UC Davis, an influential university—especially for environmental stewardship
- Mostly paved path is suitable for dogs with less mobility

Enjoy a relaxed and educational trail at the UC Davis Arboretum and Public Garden through several outdoor exhibits showcasing various flora.

UC Davis is a prominent institution and cornerstone of sustainable agriculture, sustainability, and climate-change research in Northern California. The UC Davis Arboretum and Public Garden welcomes both human and canine visitors to its 100-acre living museum to learn more about plants and agriculture. Your hike on the Arboretum Trail has multiple stops at exhibits showcasing diverse plant collections, each with interpretive signs highlighting the importance of biodiversity and conservation. Beyond its role as a public garden, the arboretum also functions as a living laboratory for students and researchers of UC Davis.

Your hike begins at the Peter J. Shields Oak Grove, named after Judge Peter J. Shields, who helped found UC Davis in 1906. The oak grove has over 80 kinds of oak, including english oak, coast live oak, and bur oak. Oaks range in height from 2 to 200 feet, showcasing remarkable variation in their appearance.

As you continue, you'll walk along the Arboretum Waterway, a controlled section of Putah Creek that helps manage water flow and supports diverse aquatic habitats. You'll reach the Mediterranean Collection about half a mile into the hike and then the Southwestern U.S. and Mexican Collection after three-quarters of a mile.

A little after a mile into the hike, you'll arrive at both the Warren G. Roberts Redbud Collection and the Native American Contemplative Garden in short succession. Redbuds are small, ornamental trees known for their striking magenta-pink blossoms in early spring. Native to California's Central Valley, redbuds are well-adapted to the region's warm and dry climate, making them a low-maintenance addition to your garden. Native tribes also used redbud shoots for woven baskets that they used for cooking and trapping fish. Your next stop at the Native American Contemplative Garden honors and recognizes the Patwin people as the original inhabitants of this land.

After you cross the street, you'll reach the Mary Wattis Brown Garden of California Native Plants and the T. Elliot Weier Redwood Grove. The California Native collection showcases native plants that provide important nutrients for native birds and insects, while the Redwood Grove showcases coastal redwoods that grow on the coast of California and southern Oregon. Then, you'll reach the Australian Collection, which features eucalyptus trees, shrubs, and perennials native to that region. After three-quarters of a mile, you'll arrive at the East Asian Collection. The open lawns here are a great place to stop for a picnic.
In the spring, you may see cherry blossoms in bloom.

TURN-BY-TURN DIRECTIONS

1. From the trailhead, head straight at the sign "Arboretum Continues." After 150 feet, turn right at the unmarked junction and pass a water fountain and restrooms.
2. At 300 feet, the Peter J. Shields Oak Grove will be on your right; continue straight.
3. At 550 feet, reach the White Flower Garden Gazebo on your left; continue straight.
4. At 0.2 miles, turn left at the unmarked junction.
5. At 0.3 miles, keep straight at the unmarked junction. Do not turn left.
6. At 0.4 miles, stay right at the unmarked junction to continue on the path. The Mediterranean Collection will be 600 feet ahead.
7. At 0.6 miles, turn right to cross the bridge. Once across the bridge, immediately turn left.
8. At 0.7 miles, turn left at the unmarked junction, crossing the river again. Once on the other side, immediately turn right to continue on the Arboretum Trail.
9. At 0.8 miles, take the trail spur on the left for a short detour off the main path to explore the Southwestern U.S. and Mexican Collection.
10. At 1.0 miles, reach the Warren G. Roberts Redbud Collection.
11. At 1.1 miles, stay right at the unmarked junction to continue on the path. The Native American Contemplative Garden will be on your right.
12. At 1.2 miles, cross Mrak Hall Drive and continue on the path toward the signposted "California Natives." After 400 feet, reach the Mary Wattis Brown Garden of California Native Plants on your right.
13. At 1.5 miles, reach Wyatt Deck on your right. Continue straight as the paved path becomes a dirt path at the T. Elliot Weier Redwood Grove.
14. At 1.7 miles, reach the Australian Collection on your left. After 300 feet, turn left onto the dirt path just before the sign for "Arboretum GATEway Garden." After 100 feet, take another left to head westward on the loop. We are heading back to the trailhead on the other side of the waterway.
15. At 2.2 miles, cross the street onto a dirt path to continue straight.
16. At 2.3 miles, continue straight as you get back onto a paved path.
17. At 2.5 miles, turn left at the unmarked junction to walk through the East Asian Collection.
18. At 2.6 miles, reach the Mrak Hall Drive intersection from Step 12 and cross the street to continue straight. From this point onward, you'll be retracing your steps back to Step 5.
19. At 3.6 miles, reach the intersection from Step 5 and turn right at the unmarked path to head away from the waterway and back to the trailhead.
20. At 3.7 miles, turn right to reach the trailhead, 200 feet ahead.

SHASTA COUNTY

MOUNT SHASTA
P
1
Castle Lake
4
3
2

P Parking

ft
7000
6500
6000
5500
5000
0.0
0.5
1.0
1.5
2.0
2.5
3.0 mi

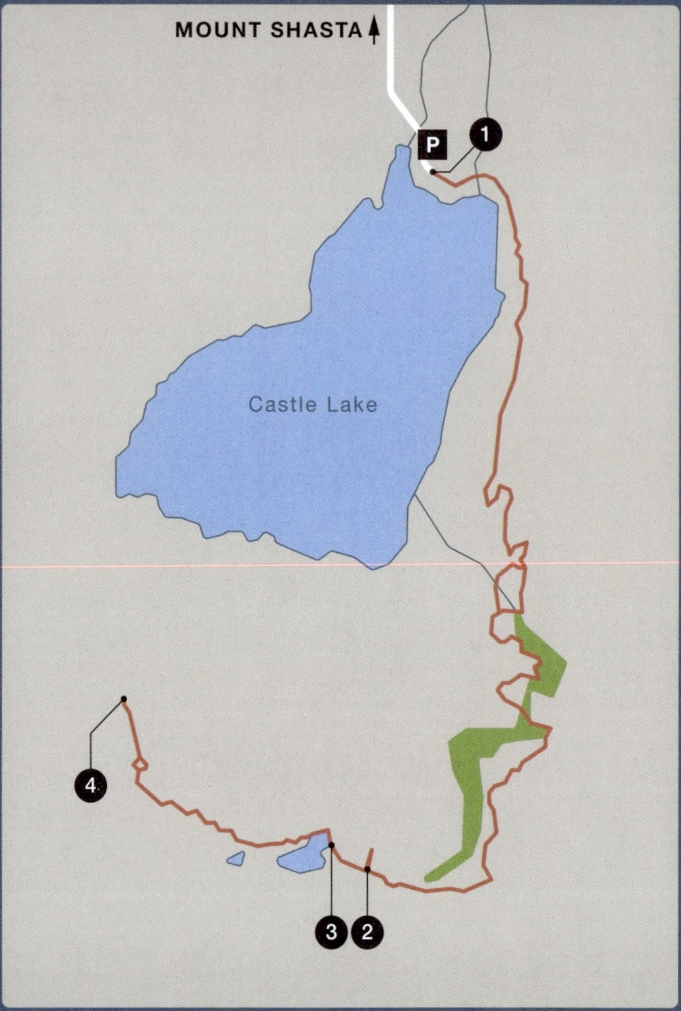

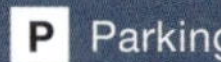

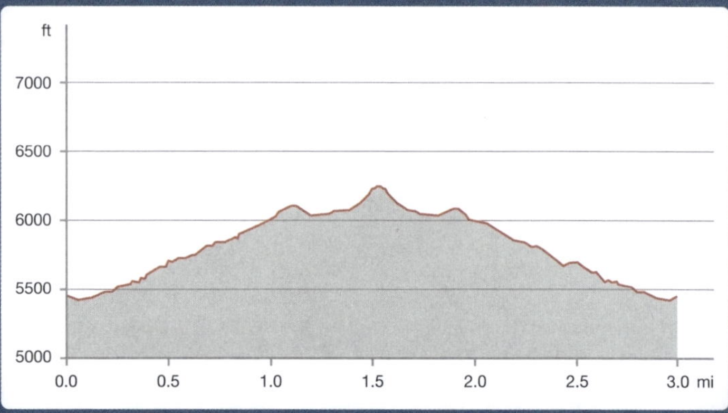

HEART LAKE

STUNNING VIEWS OF MOUNT SHASTA

DUNSMUIR, CA

38

LENGTH
3 miles
(loop)

TIME & MONEY
2 hours,
free

ELEVATION GAIN
794 feet

DIFFICULTY
Moderate

CONDITIONS
Year-round; snowshoes may be required in the winter, mostly exposed

HIGHLIGHTS
Alpine lakes, mountain views

ESSENTIALS

- **Find the trailhead:** From Redding, take Interstate 5 North toward Portland. In 58 miles, take the exit for CA-89 South toward McCloud. In 0.3 miles, merge onto CA-89 South. In 0.1 miles, turn right onto Big Canyon Drive. In 0.3 miles, turn right onto Azalea Drive. In 0.4 miles, turn right onto South Old Stage Road. In 1.1 miles, turn left onto Siskiyou Lake Boulevard. In 0.9 miles, turn left onto West A Barr Road. In 0.9 miles, turn left onto Ney Springs Road. In 0.1 miles, continue straight onto Castle Lake Road. The parking lot is at the end of Castle Lake Road, 7.1 miles ahead.
- **Land manager:** USDA Forest Service—Mount Shasta Ranger Station (fs.usda.gov/stnf)

WHY YOU'LL LOVE IT

- Jaw-dropping views of Mount Shasta
- Lakes for dogs to swim in
- Stunning mountain views for relatively low effort

Hike past Castle Lake and Heart Lake to the top of Castle Lake Viewpoint, where on a clear day, you'll be rewarded with views of Mount Shasta.

Mount Shasta is an outdoor-lover's paradise located in the very northern region of California, just 60 miles from the California-Oregon border. Many of the trails in Mount Shasta offer stunning alpine scenery and views of the 14,179-foot peak. In fact, President Theodore Roosevelt once declared, "I consider the evening twilight on Mount Shasta one of the grandest sights I have ever witnessed."

However, there is more to Mount Shasta than just hiking—the mountain has inspired stories and legends of the spiritual energy surrounding the region. Native American legends from the Shasta, Modoc, Atsugewi, and Wintu tribes speak of spirits or powerful beings connected to Mount Shasta. Today, spiritual-minded visitors come to Mount Shasta for the energy vortexes that connect mind and spirit.

Even if you're not spiritual, this hike will reward you with beautiful mountain scenery from start to finish. For the first half mile on your way up to Castle Lake Viewpoint, you'll follow the eastern edge of Castle Lake. This is the larger of the two lakes at 47 acres of surface area and up to 120 feet deep. As you climb higher in elevation, you may see some fishermen below, as the lake is home to a variety of trout species, including rainbow, brook, and brown trout.

After less than a mile along the gently inclining path, you'll reach a small peak with a good vantage point of Castle Lake and Mount Shasta. If your dogs have mobility issues, this is an easier vantage point than our final destination, as the climb to Castle Lake Viewpoint requires a bit of scrambling. A couple of hundred feet after this vantage point, you'll pass Heart Lake, a much smaller heart-shaped lake nestled between rocky cliffs. Heart Lake is a bit muddier because of its smaller size, but your dogs can still swim in the lake.

The final stretch of your hike to the top is unmarked and scrambles over boulders. While tricky, it's manageable for most dogs. On a clear day, you'll see an incredible view of Mount Shasta beaming behind Castle Lake. Mount Shasta has a snow-capped peak for most of the year due to its high elevation at 14,179 feet.

TURN-BY-TURN DIRECTIONS

1. From the trailhead, follow the sign to Heart Lake.
2. At 1.1 miles, reach a small peak on your right. Climb to the top for a vantage point of Castle Lake below. When you're ready, head back down the small peak and continue straight on the Heart Lake Trail.
3. At 1.2 miles, reach Heart Lake. After enjoying the lake, the unmarked trail continues straight past Heart Lake, up to Castle Lake Viewpoint.
4. At 1.6 miles, reach Castle Lake Viewpoint. This is the end of the trail. Retrace your steps to head back to the parking lot, where there are vault toilets.

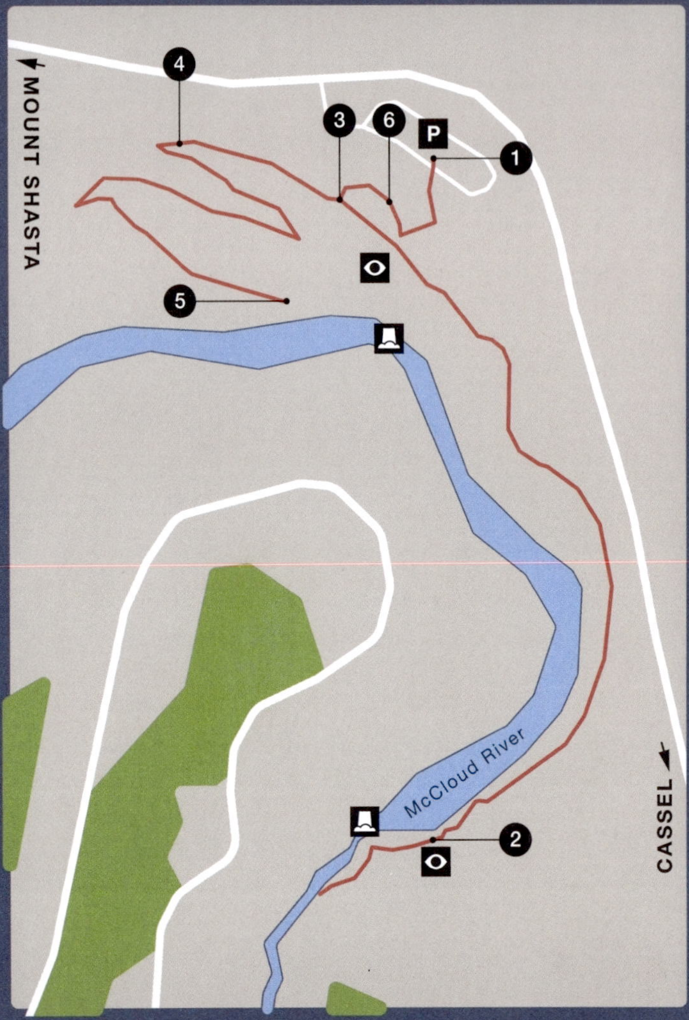

MOUNT SHASTA
CASSEL
McCloud River
1
2
3
4
5
6
P

P Parking
Waterfall
Viewpoint

ft
4000
3500
3000
2500
2000
0.0
0.5
1.0
1.5
1.8 mi

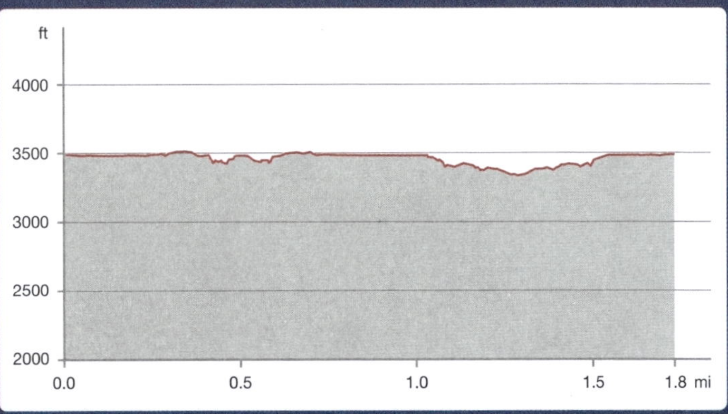

UPPER AND MIDDLE MCCLOUD FALLS

DISCOVER WATERFALLS IN SHASTA

MCCLOUD, CA

39

LENGTH
1.8 miles (loop)

TIME & MONEY
1 hour, free

ELEVATION GAIN
157 feet

DIFFICULTY
Easy

CONDITIONS
April–November; exposed, stairs

HIGHLIGHTS
Waterfalls, interpretive signs

ESSENTIALS

- **Find the trailhead:** From Redding, take Interstate 5 North toward Portland. In 57.8 miles, exit onto CA-89 South / Volcanic Legacy Scenic Byway toward McCloud. In 0.3 miles, merge onto CA-89 South. In 15.2 miles, turn right onto Fowler Public Camp Road. In 0.6 miles, turn left at the sign for Middle Falls and Upper Falls. In 0.9 miles, the parking lot will be on your right.

- **Land manager:** USDA Forest Service—McCloud Ranger Station (fs.usda.gov/stnf)

WHY YOU'LL LOVE IT

- Scenic waterfalls
- Dogs can wade in the water at Middle Falls
- Educational interpretive signs at Upper Falls

Hike to the cascading Upper Falls and Middle Falls, tucked into a lush canyon of the McCloud River.

The McCloud River is a stunning 77-mile river that flows through the Mount Shasta area. This hike takes you to Upper and Middle Falls, while skipping the awkward hiking portion of Lower Falls, where you'd need to cross through a campground.

The McCloud Falls area gets many of its geologic characteristics from Mount Shasta's previous volcanic activity. The water runs through volcanic rocks, including basalt, which comes from ancient lava flows. You may be able to see sections of columnar basalt, which is formed when volcanic rocks cool into rough prismatic patterns.

You'll reach the Middle Falls Viewpoint a couple hundred feet after leaving the parking lot. From here, you'll have a broad view of Middle Falls and the surrounding river scenery from 100 feet up. Forests of pine trees like Douglas fir and white fir, and other plants like Pacific dogwood, surround the McCloud River. In the fall, all but the pines change to vibrant reds, oranges, and yellows, putting on a colorful show for leaf-peepers.

Your next stop is Upper Falls, where you'll reach an ADA accessible paved area that traces along the river. At Upper Falls, look out for interpretive signs, which provide interesting information about the history and surrounding area. For instance, the Upper Falls were home to Native peoples, mostly notably the Winnemem Wintu, Shasta, and Pit River Tribes who lived near the falls for thousands of years before European settlers displaced them.

Over the next quarter mile, you'll have multiple vantage points to look down below into Upper Falls and McCloud River. Looking upstream from the falls, you'll see how the water has carved through the volcanic rock over time, and ultimately pushes out through a channel in the basalt wall to form Upper Falls. As you walk along the riverbank around Upper Falls, look out for crops of umbrella plants. Aptly named, the umbrella plant has large, umbrella-like leaves that help keep the surrounding area cool and moist. The umbrella plant also helps stabilize the surrounding soil and prevents erosion.

After leaving Upper Falls, you'll take the same trail back to Middle Falls Viewpoint and continue straight to head down to Middle Falls. There's a short section of stairs here that can be tougher for dogs with mobility issues. At 50 feet wide, Middle Falls is your grand finale. The cascading, dramatic waterfall is incredibly picturesque and flows into a slower section in the river. The slower water after Middle Falls is a great opportunity for your dogs to dip their feet into the water and cool off.

TURN-BY-TURN DIRECTIONS

1. From the parking lot, head onto the paved trail at the Middle McCloud Falls sign. After 175 feet, reach Middle Falls Viewpoint, where you can see Middle Falls below. Continue southeast on the McCloud Waterfalls Trail toward Upper Falls. (If you're facing the river, you'll be heading left. We will return to this junction in Step 3.)
2. At 0.4 miles, reach Upper Falls. There are multiple vantage points of the falls along the railing. When you're ready, turn around and head back toward the Middle Falls Viewpoint.
3. At 0.9 miles, instead of continuing on the unmarked paved trail back to Middle Falls Viewpoint, turn left on an unmarked dirt path along the canyon wall that we passed in Step 1. You're heading down into the canyon to Middle Falls.
4. At 1.0 miles, continue straight down the set of wooden stairs.
5. At 1.3 miles, reach Middle Falls. You can scramble down the rocks to reach the water, where your dogs can cool off. When you're ready, head back up the way you came.
6. At 1.7 miles, reach the junction from Step 3. Stay left on the unmarked paved trail back to the parking lot, where there are bear-proof trash bins and a vault toilet.

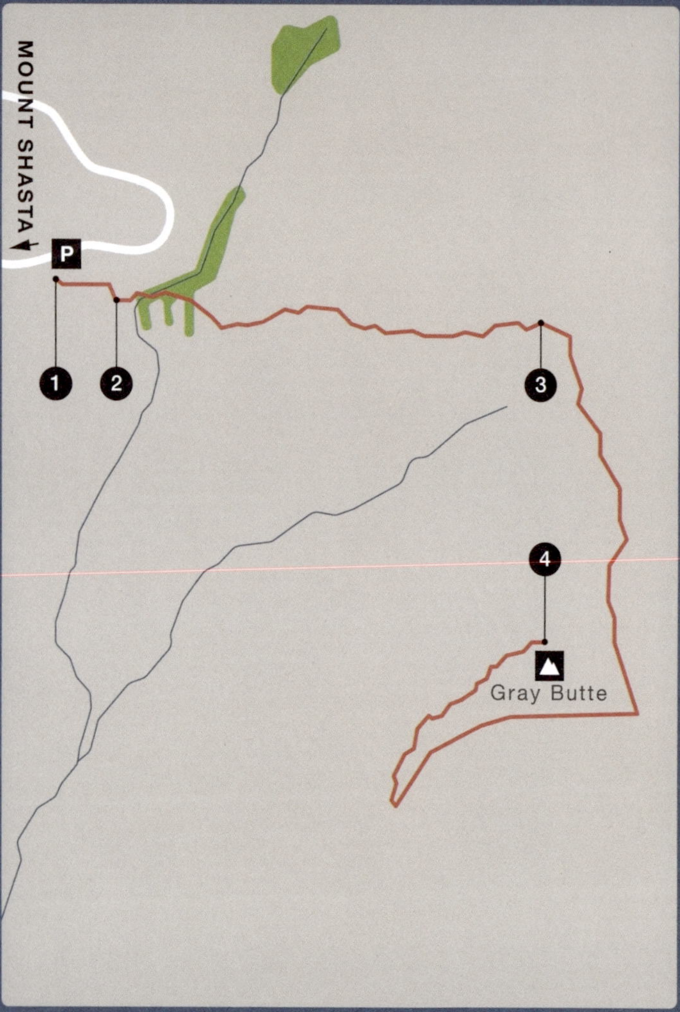

MOUNT SHASTA

P

1

2

3

4

Gray Butte

P Parking

Gray Butte

GRAY BUTTE

SUMMIT GRAY BUTTE FOR MOUNT SHASTA VIEWS

MCCLOUD, CA

40

LENGTH
3.3 miles
(loop)

TIME & MONEY
2 hours,
free

ELEVATION GAIN
609 feet

DIFFICULTY
Moderate

CONDITIONS
July–November;
exposed, sunny

HIGHLIGHTS
Mountain views,
alpine meadow

ESSENTIALS

- **Find the trailhead:** From Redding, take Interstate 5 North toward Portland. In 60 miles, take the exit for W Lake Street. In 0.2 miles, turn right onto W Lake Street. In 0.4 miles, continue straight onto E Lake Street. In 0.4 miles, take a slight left to N Washington Drive. In 0.1 miles, continue onto County Highway A10. In 12.7 miles, arrive at the parking lot for Panther Meadows Campground on your right.
- **Land manager:** USDA Forest Service—Mount Shasta Ranger Station (fs.usda.gov/stnf)

WHY YOU'LL LOVE IT

- Well-maintained trail for dogs' paws
- View of Mount Shasta
- Small creek running through meadows

Hike through the grassy Panther Meadows and up to the Gray Butte summit, where you'll be rewarded with south-side views of Mount Shasta.

Your adventure to Gray Butte begins on the Everitt Memorial Highway, a stunning mountain road that climbs 4,300 feet over 14 miles. Everitt Memorial Highway is named in honor of John S. Everitt, a forest supervisor for the Shasta National Forest. The highway pays tribute to John's sacrifice to Mount Shasta and the Forest Service, as he sadly died while taking on a solo investigation of the Bear Springs Wildfire in 1934.

The Gray Butte Trail starts at the exit for Panther Meadows Campground, one of the last exits before the end of the Everitt Memorial Highway. This gives you a great opportunity to peek out your window at the different viewpoints of Mount Shasta as you drive up the mountain road. There are many stops along the twists and turns of Everitt Memorial Highway, including the Bunny Flat area, Old Ski Bowl, and finally Panther Meadows. Due to wilderness regulations, dogs are not allowed on many of the hikes off of Everitt Memorial Highway. However, they are allowed on the Gray Butte Trail.

You'll begin your hike by going through Panther Meadows, a lush meadow that sits at 7,600 feet elevation. The meadow is home to sensitive plants like alpine laurel and mountain heather, both of which are extremely vulnerable to being stepped on or otherwise broken. Mountain heather can take 200 to 400 years to reach its full shrub height! Because of the sensitive habitat, the officials at Shasta–Trinity National Forest issued an order in 2024 tightening restrictions on parking, camping, and maximum group sizes. Part of that restriction requires that dogs are leashed to avoid accidental trampling of sensitive plants.

Once you leave Panther Meadows, the environment changes from small shrubbery in the meadows to hundred-feet-tall Shasta red firs and mountain hemlocks. You'll also pass through larger rocks and boulders along the Gray Butte Trail that are more typical of subalpine conditions in Shasta.

Shasta red fir is a variety of California red fir that is found in higher elevations. It has a red-brown tree trunk and short, dark-green needles that point upwards from its branches. Its cones are cylindrical and may look shaggy because its bracts (bracts are like a tiny leaf that sits at the base of the cone) are longer than its scales.

Around a mile into the hike, you'll see fewer red firs and more hemlock trees. Because hemlocks grow at higher elevations, their branches are stiff and droop down to shed snow. They generally grow to around one hundred feet, and their trunks have purples and grays mixed with the brown bark. The hemlocks start to thin out near the top of the Gray Butte summit, where a clearing makes way for impressive south-side views of Mount Shasta.

TURN-BY-TURN DIRECTIONS

1. From the parking lot, take the trail marked by a small sign noted as "trail."
2. At 0.1 miles, reach the Panther Meadows Trailhead. Take the trail to the left of the campsite signage. After 100 feet, keep right to get on the signposted Gray Butte Trail.
3. At 0.6 miles, keep right to continue on the signposted Gray Butte Trail.
4. At 1.7 miles, reach the top of Gray Butte. Enjoy the 360-degree views, and when you're ready, retrace your steps back to the parking lot.

MENDOCINO COAST

FORT BRAGG

SANTA ROSA

MENDOCINO

P Parking

Picnic table

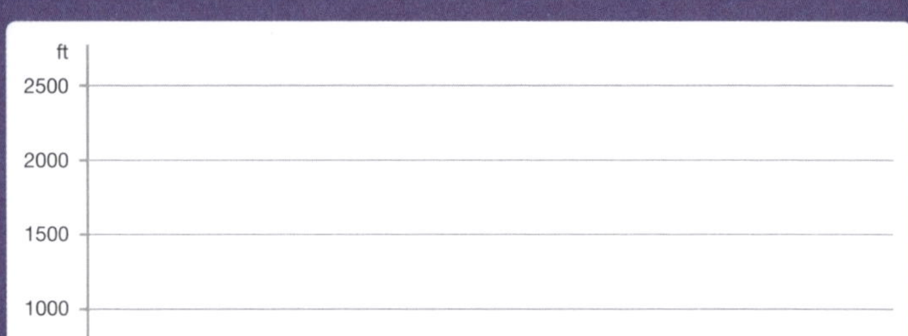

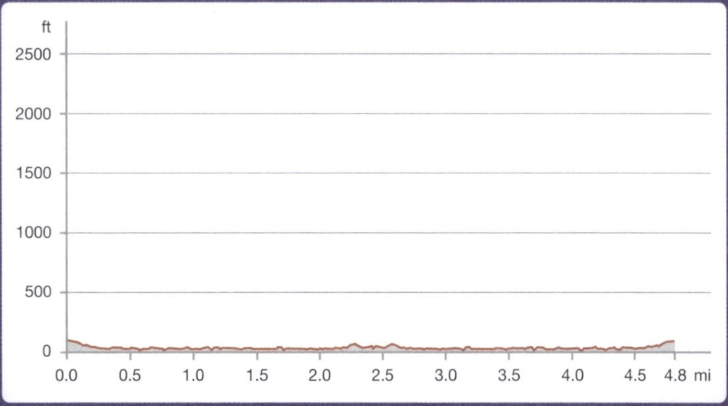

MENDOCINO HEADLANDS STATE PARK

HIKE RUGGED BLUFFS NEAR A SEASIDE TOWN

MENDOCINO, CA

41

LENGTH
4.8 miles (round trip)

TIME & MONEY
2 hours, free

ELEVATION GAIN
275 feet

DIFFICULTY
Moderate

CONDITIONS
Year-round; exposed, coastal weather

HIGHLIGHTS
Coastal views, cypress grove

ESSENTIALS

- **Find the trailhead:** From Geyserville, continue on US-101 north for 10.0 miles and then take the exit for CA-128 west toward Fort Bragg/Mendocino. In 0.2 miles, turn left onto CA-128 west and then in 0.8 miles, keep right to stay on CA-128 west. In 55.4 miles, continue onto CA-1 north. In 10.2 miles, turn left onto Main Street and continue for 0.4 miles. Park along Main Street near the Ford House Museum. The museum is open every day from 11 a.m.–4 p.m.

- **Land manager:** California State Parks (parks.ca.gov)

WHY YOU'LL LOVE IT

- Spectacular sea arches and offshore rock formations
- Experience a seaside Victorian town and its visitor center
- Flexible trail distance accommodates dogs of varying abilities

Follow dramatic coastal bluffs around the historic Mendocino village, discovering sea arches and carved totem poles before reaching the Cypress Grove and Point Kelli overlook.

Mendocino Headlands State Park hugs the charming village of Mendocino. Pioneers founded Mendocino in 1852 at the height of the lumber industry, when the town bustled with lumber mills and shipping points. Lumber workers loaded redwood logs onto "doghole schooners" – small sailing vessels that navigated the treacherous coast of Northern California by ducking into inlets that larger boats couldn't access.

Your coastal stroll begins at the Ford House Museum. Jerome B. Ford was the superintendent of Mendocino's first sawmill. He is also widely credited as the town's founder. Inside the museum, you'll find fascinating exhibits that showcase Mendocino's history, although they do not allow dogs inside.

Around half a mile in, you'll see Portuguese Beach down a set of sandy steps. If your dog struggles to navigate steep steps, you can skip this detour and enjoy the views from the bluffs instead. Otherwise, take the steps down to Portuguese Beach, where you can explore tide pools at low tide. After you're done exploring, you'll take the steps back up to the bluffs. The trail then narrows into a single track along the coast as you pass totem poles carved by locals.

After the beach, you'll get to a parking lot with a commemorative plaque with both Japanese and English text. The plaque is a dedication to Mendocino's sister city, Miasa, Japan, and their ongoing student and art exchange programs. As you continue through the parking lot, you'll see the Mendocino arch and Goat Island rising from the ocean.

After the Mendocino arch, the trail follows alongside Heeser Drive north. You may see cars passing as you continue to the north side of the park. In the spring, the coastal prairie bursts into color with orange California poppies, purple lupine, and lavender-colored seaside daisies. While peak bloom times vary by species, wildflowers tend to last until the end of summer.

Around a mile and a half into the hike, you'll reach Point Yoav. In the early summer, you may see Brandt's cormorants and common murres nesting on the rocks ahead. Finally, you'll arrive at Cypress Grove. This peaceful grove has tall Monterey cypress trees that provide shelter from the coastal winds. The shaded area offers a quiet contrast to the exposed bluffs. At the end of Cypress Grove, you'll reach Point Kelli, a scenic overlook with views to the further Russian Gulch and Point Cabrillo Light Station (covered in the next chapter). From Point Kelli, you'll retrace your steps back to the trailhead.

TURN-BY-TURN DIRECTIONS

1. From the Ford House Museum, head past the gravel road and toward the coast to get onto the main trail.
2. At 0.1 miles, turn right onto the unmarked trail.
3. At 0.2 miles, continue straight on the unmarked Mendocino Headlands Bluff Trail, ignoring the trail on your right.
4. At 0.3 miles, turn left at the unmarked junction to stay on the Mendocino Headlands Bluff Trail, hugging the coast.
5. At 0.4 miles, turn left at the unmarked junction to continue hugging the coast. After 200 feet, there is a sign to your left marked "Trail," which leads down to Portuguese Beach. After enjoying the beach, head back up the same stairs to continue on the main trail.
6. At 0.5 miles, pass carved totem poles as the trail wraps around the bluff.
7. At 0.7 miles, continue straight at the unmarked junction, ignoring the trail on your right. Over the next 0.1 miles, there are several small unmarked trails to your right. Ignore these and continue hugging the coast on the Mendocino Headlands Bluff Trail.
8. At 1.2 miles, pass a commemorative plaque and then cross through the parking lot. The unmarked trail continues on the other side of the parking lot.
9. At 1.3 miles, continue following the unmarked trail around a second parking lot.
10. At 1.6 miles, turn left to continue hugging the coast on the unmarked trail.
11. At 1.8 miles, arrive at Point Yoav. Continue straight on the unmarked trail, passing behind a third parking lot.
12. At 2.2 miles, arrive at the Cypress Grove parking area, where there are restrooms, trash bins, a water spigot, and picnic tables. Turn left into Cypress Grove.
13. At 2.3 miles, arrive at Point Kelli. Retrace your steps to return to the trailhead.

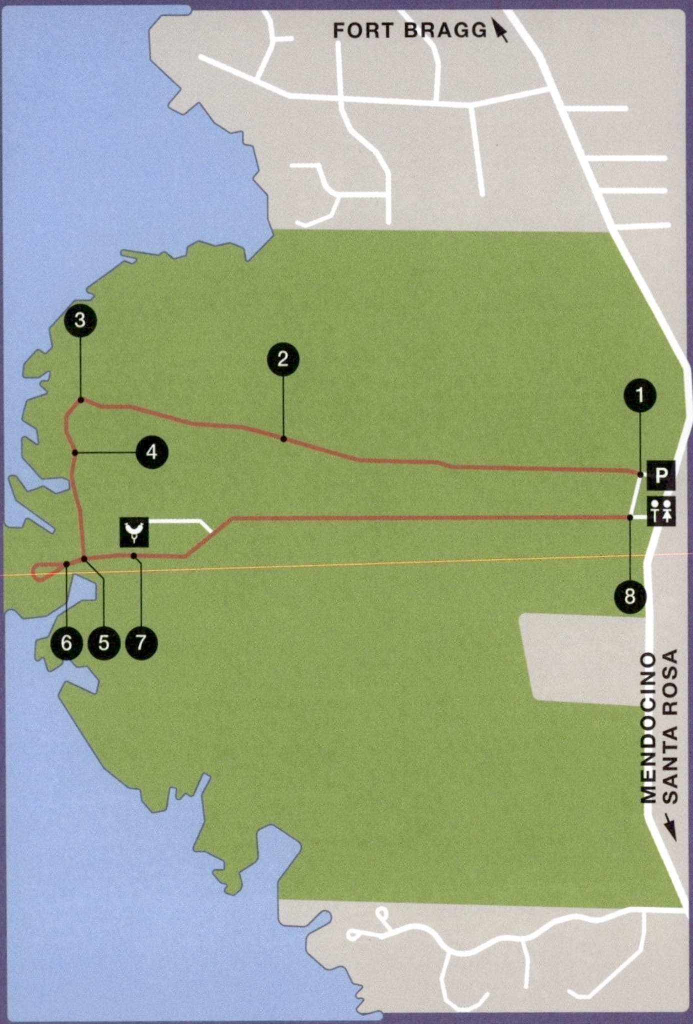

FORT BRAGG
1
2
3
4
5
6
7
8
P
MENDOCINO
SANTA ROSA

P Parking · Toilet · Picnic table

ft
2500
2000
1500
1000
500
0
0.0
0.5
1.0
1.5
1.7 mi

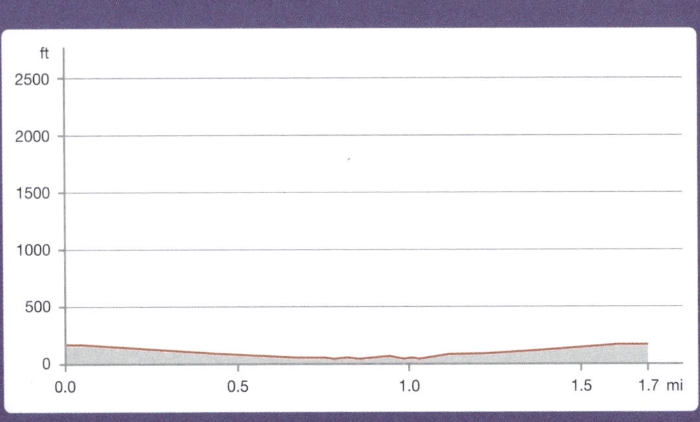

POINT CABRILLO LIGHT STATION

VISIT A HISTORIC LIGHTHOUSE ON THE COAST

MENDOCINO, CA

42

LENGTH
1.7 miles (loop)

TIME & MONEY
1 hour, free

ELEVATION GAIN
117 feet

DIFFICULTY
Easy

CONDITIONS
Year-round; mostly exposed, museums open 11 a.m.–4 p.m.

HIGHLIGHTS
Historic lighthouse, coastal views

ESSENTIALS

- **Find the trailhead:** From the Ford House Museum in Mendocino, head east on Main Street and continue for 0.1 miles. At the intersection with Howard Street, turn left. In 0.2 miles, turn right onto Little Lake Road. After 0.1 miles, turn left onto CA-1 north. Stay on CA-1 north for 1.7 miles, then turn left onto Brest Road for Point Cabrillo Light Station. After 150 feet, turn right onto Point Cabrillo Drive. In 1.2 miles, turn left onto Lighthouse Road to enter the parking lot, where there are restrooms and trash bins.

- **Land manager:** California State Parks (parks.ca.gov)

WHY YOU'LL LOVE IT

- Active lighthouse
- Well-maintained historic buildings and museums
- Gentle paths suitable for dogs of all ages

Stroll to the charming Point Cabrillo Light Station and learn about how the lighthouse operates, its history, and the nearby marine life.

Point Cabrillo Light Station sits on a 270-acre headland in Mendocino. The lighthouse was built in 1909 to provide crucial navigation aid for small "doghole" schooners that transported lumber from Mendocino's mills (see the Mendocino Headlands State Park chapter). You'll begin your journey walking through grassland and coastal prairie. You may spot black-tailed deer grazing among the grasses. As keystone species, black-tailed deer play a crucial role in maintaining the area's ecosystem. The grassland is a prime area for ticks, so keep your dog on the trail.

About a mile in, you'll arrive at the Point Cabrillo Light Station. All the buildings on the grounds permit well-behaved and leashed dogs. To your right, you'll see a charming building with a bright-red roof and cedar shingles. This is the restored Blacksmith & Carpentry Shop, which houses the Marine Science Exhibit. You can explore a saltwater aquarium inside and learn more about the coastal ecosystem.

Across from the Marine Science Exhibit, you'll find the Point Cabrillo Lighthouse and Museum. Inside, you'll see examples of the equipment that scientists use to illuminate and turn the massive Fresnel lens—an important technology that transformed maritime navigation by enlarging and intensifying light beams. After exploring the various educational exhibits, you can browse the shared gift shop and (optionally) contribute to a donation bin to support the museum's restoration efforts.

After you leave the lighthouse, you'll see the historic lightkeeper residences. The first two houses on your left are the Second Assistant Lightkeeper's House and the Head Lightkeeper's House. They are now vacation rentals, and you may see visitors enjoying the views on their porches. The third building is the First Assistant Lightkeeper's House. Now a museum, the interior reflects how the house would have looked in the 1930s and features displays about the Keepers' duties, along with photographs of those who once lived there.

Your return to the parking lot is on a paved road. Volunteers added educational signs about gray whales along the road. Although the signs are for younger kids, they're still a fun read. Every year, Eastern Pacific gray whales migrate past Point Cabrillo traveling between food sources in the Arctic and the safe lagoons in Baja for breeding. You'll have the best chance of seeing gray whales along the coast from December into April.

TURN-BY-TURN DIRECTIONS

1. From the parking lot, take the Point Cabrillo Light Station Trail on the right of the signpost. After 100 feet, continue straight at the unmarked junction.
2. At 0.4 miles, continue straight at the marked junction toward the light station.
3. At 0.7 miles, turn left at the unmarked fork.
4. At 0.8 miles, keep right at the unmarked fork.
5. At 0.9 miles, turn right to reach the Point Cabrillo Light Station area. Explore the Marine Science Exhibit in the restored Blacksmith & Carpentry Shop to your right and the Point Cabrillo Lighthouse straight ahead.
6. When you're ready, head away from the lighthouse on the paved road, ignoring the unmarked trail on the left that you came from.
7. At 1.1 miles, arrive at a cluster of historic buildings with picnic tables on your left. The first two houses are the Second Assistant Lightkeeper's House and Head Lightkeeper's House, which are now vacation rentals. The third building—originally the First Assistant Lightkeeper's House—is now a museum. Continue straight on the paved Lighthouse Road, ignoring a road that goes left to a parking lot.
8. At 1.7 miles, arrive back at the parking lot.

ACKNOWLEDGMENTS

Thank you to my friends and hiking companions over the years. From summiting the New Hampshire 4,000-footers to enduring heavy rain on the Laugavegur Trail to hiking 20+ miles a day with 35-pound packs on the Tour du Mont Blanc (because we wanted to wear dresses and makeup for nice dinners), the memories we made together have shaped my love for hiking.

Deepest gratitude to the land managers, park employees, volunteers, and outdoor advocates whose tireless dedication preserves and protects these wild spaces for all to experience.

I'm endlessly grateful to Ty and Gus, the best dogs and hiking companions a person could ask for. They get excited for every adventure and always keep me company on road trips. Hiking with them has made my journey in the outdoors so much richer.

My early hiking experiences were shaped by my parents, who took me on fun camping and hiking adventures when I was young. Those foundational memories sparked everything that followed.

Finally, thank you to my husband, Shai, who not only supported me during this journey but solo-parented our two young kids while I went off hiking with the dogs. His encouragement made this book possible.

I owe a big thank you to the team at Helvetiq. My editor Johanna Flashman, who led the way with her support and insightful feedback. She remained both patient and discerning as I translated my thoughts and ideas into words. Richard Harvell, for reaching out to me and setting me on this rewarding journey of authorship. Elżbieta Kownacka, whose beautiful illustrations and thoughtful design brought these pages to life. And to Jill McMahon and Kristen Valenti, authors of *Dog Hiking New England*, who helped pave the way.

Melissa Chen
August 2025

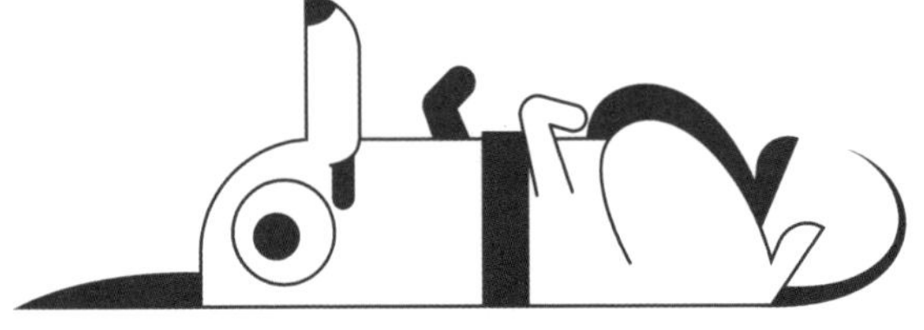